The Mass

The Catholic Order of Mass

Acknowledgements:

All scriptures and readings are taken from the Douay-Rheims Catholic Bible.

Table of Content

Introductory Rites

The Liturgy of the Word

The Liturgy of the Eucharist

The Concluding Rites

Introductory Rites

The Introductory Rites help the faithful come together as one, establish communion and prepare themselves properly to listen to the Word of God and to celebrate the Eucharist worthily.

All stand. The Priest approaches the altar with the ministers and venerates it while the Entrance Song is sung

Sign of the Cross

All make the Sign of the Cross as the Priest says.

In the name of the Father, and of the Son, and of the Holy Spirit.

The people reply:

Amen.

Greeting

Then the Priest greets the people:

Either: The grace of our Lord Jesus Christ,

and the love of God,

and the communion of the Holy Spirit

be with you all.

Or: Grace to you and peace from God our Father

and the Lord Jesus Christ.

Or: The Lord be with you.

1

The people reply:

And with your spirit.

The Priest, or a Deacon, or another minister, may very briefly introduce the faithful to the Mass of the day.

Penitential Act

The Priest invites the faithful to the Penitential Act.

Brethren (brothers and sisters), let us acknowledge our sins,

and so prepare ourselves to celebrate the sacred mysteries.

A brief pause for silence follows, and then one of the following Penitential Acts:

A

All say:

I confess to almighty God

and to you, my brothers and sisters,

that I have greatly sinned,

in my thoughts and in my words,

in what I have done and in what I have failed to do,

And, striking their breast, they say:

through my fault,

through my fault,

through my most grievous fault;

therefore I ask blessed Mary ever-Virgin,

all the Angels and Saints,

and you, my brothers and sisters,

to pray for me to the Lord our God.

The absolution by the Priest follows:

May almighty God have mercy on us,

forgive us our sins,

and bring us to everlasting life.

Amen.

The Kyrie

The Kyrie, eleison (Lord, have mercy) invocations may follow:

V. Lord, have mercy.

R. Lord, have mercy.

V. Christ, have mercy.

R. Christ, have mercy.

V. Lord, have mercy.

R. Lord, have mercy.

Or

V. Kyrie, eleison.

R. Kyrie, eleison.

V. Christe, eleison.

R. Christe, eleison.

V. Kyrie, eleison.

R. Kyrie, eleison.

B

The Priest says:

Have mercy on us, O Lord.

The people reply:

For we have sinned against you.

The Priest:

Show us, O Lord, your mercy.

The people:

And grant us your salvation.

The absolution by the Priest follows:

May almighty God have mercy on us,

forgive us our sins,

and bring us to everlasting life.

Amen.

The Kyrie

The Kyrie, eleison (Lord, have mercy) invocations may follow:

V. Lord, have mercy.

R. Lord, have mercy.

V. Christ, have mercy.

R. Christ, have mercy.

V. Lord, have mercy.

R. Lord, have mercy.

Or

V. Kyrie, eleison.

R. Kyrie, eleison.

V. Christe, eleison.

R. Christe, eleison.

V. Kyrie, eleison.

R. Kyrie, eleison.

C

The Priest or another minister says invocations naming the gracious works of the Lord to which he invites the people to respond, as in the example below:

You were sent to heal the contrite of heart:

Lord, have mercy. Or: Kyrie, eleison.

The people reply:

Lord, have mercy. Or: Kyrie, eleison.

The Priest:

You came to call sinners:

Christ, have mercy. Or: Christe, eleison.

The people:

Christ, have mercy. Or: Christe, eleison.

The Priest:

You are seated at the right hand of the Father to intercede for us:

Lord, have mercy. Or: Kyrie, eleison.

The people:

Lord, have mercy. Or: Kyrie, eleison.

The absolution by the Priest follows:

May almighty God have mercy on us,

forgive us our sins, and bring us to everlasting life.

Amen.

The Gloria

When indicated this hymn is either sung or said.

Glory to God in the highest,

and on earth peace to people of good will.

We praise you,

we bless you,

we adore you,

we glorify you,

we give you thanks for your great glory,

Lord God, heavenly King,

O God, almighty Father.

Lord Jesus Christ, Only Begotten Son,

Lord God, Lamb of God, Son of the Father,

you take away the sins of the world,

have mercy on us;

you take away the sins of the world,

receive our prayer;

you are seated at the right hand of the Father,

have mercy on us.

For you alone are the Holy One,

you alone are the Lord,

you alone are the Most High,

Jesus Christ,

with the Holy Spirit,

in the glory of God the Father.

Amen.

The Collect

The Priest says:

Let us pray.

And all pray in silence with the Priest for a while. Then the Priest says the Collect prayer, at the end of which the people acclaim:

Amen.

The Liturgy of the Word

By hearing the word proclaimed in worship, the faithful again enter into the unending dialogue between God and the covenant people, a dialogue sealed in the sharing of the Eucharistic food and drink. The proclamation of the word is thus integral to the Mass and at its very centre. It is appropriate to have a brief time of quiet after the readings for those present to take the word of God to heart and begin to prepare a prayerful response to what they have heard.

All sit

First Reading

To indicate the end of these readings, the reader acclaims:

The word of the Lord.

All reply:

Thanks be to God.

Psalm

After the First Reading the psalmist or cantor sings or says the Psalm, with the people making the response.

Second Reading

On Sundays and certain other days there is a second reading. It concludes with the same responsory as above.

Gospel

The assembly stands to sing the Gospel Acclamation to welcome the Gospel. They remain standing in honour of the Gospel reading, the high point of the Liturgy of the Word. At the ambo the Deacon, or the Priest says:

The Lord be with you.

The people reply:

And with your spirit.

The Deacon, or the Priest:

A reading from the holy Gospel according to N.

He makes the Sign of the Cross on the book and, together with the people, on his forehead, lips, and breast. At the same time the people acclaim:

Glory to you, O Lord.

At the end of the Gospel, the Deacon, or the Priest, acclaims:

The Gospel of the Lord.

All reply:

Praise to you, Lord Jesus Christ.

After the proclamation of the Gospel the congregation is seated.

The Homily

At the end of the Homily it is appropriate for there to be a brief silence for recollection. The congregation then stands.

The Creed

On Sundays and Solemnities, the Profession of Faith or Creed will follow. During Lent and Easter Time, especially, the Apostles' Creed may be used.

Niceno-Constantinopolitan ("Nicen") Creed

The Niceno-Constantinopolitan Creed

I believe in one God,

the Father almighty,

maker of heaven and earth,

of all things visible and invisible.

I believe in one Lord Jesus Christ,

the Only Begotten Son of God,

born of the Father before all ages.

God from God,

Light from Light,

true God from true God,

begotten, not made, consubstantial with the Father;

through him all things were made.

For us men and for our salvation he came down from heaven,

At the words that follow, up to and including 'and became man', all bow.

and by the Holy Spirit was incarnate of the Virgin Mary,

and became man.

11

For our sake he was crucified under Pontius Pilate,

he suffered death and was buried,

and rose again on the third day

in accordance with the Scriptures.

He ascended into heaven

and is seated at the right hand of the Father.

He will come again in glory

to judge the living and the dead

and his kingdom will have no end.

I believe in the Holy Spirit, the Lord, the giver of life,

who proceeds from the Father and the Son,

who with the Father and the Son is adored and glorified,

who has spoken through the prophets.

I believe in one, holy, catholic and apostolic Church.

I confess one Baptism for the forgiveness of sins

and I look forward to the resurrection of the dead

and the life of the world to come. Amen.

Or

The Apostles' Creed

I believe in God,

the Father almighty,

Creator of heaven and earth,

and in Jesus Christ, his only Son, our Lord,

At the words that follow, up to and including 'the Virgin
Mary', all bow.

who was conceived by the Holy Spirit,

born of the Virgin Mary,

suffered under Pontius Pilate,

was crucified, died and was buried;

he descended into hell;

on the third day he rose again from the dead;

he ascended into heaven,

and is seated at the right hand of God the Father almighty;

from there he will come to judge the living and the dead.

I believe in the Holy Spirit,

the holy catholic Church,

the communion of saints,

the forgiveness of sins,

the resurrection of the body,

and life everlasting. Amen.

The Prayer of the Faithful (Bidding Prayers)

After each intention there is a pause while the faithful pray. The minister says:

Lord, in your mercy.

All reply:

Hear our prayer.

The Priest concludes the Prayer with a collect. When the Liturgy of the Word has been completed, the people sit.

The Liturgy of the Eucharist

For Catholics, the Eucharist is the source and summit of the whole Christian life. It is the vital center of all that the Church is and does, because at its heart is the real presence of the crucified, risen and glorified Lord, continuing and making available his saving work among us.

The Offertory

During the Offertory Song the faithful usually express their participation by making an offering, bringing forward bread and wine for the celebration of the Eucharist and perhaps other gifts to relieve the needs of the Church and of the poor.

When he has received the bread and wine for the celebration, the Priest offers prayer of blessing quietly at the altar. Sometimes these prayers are said aloud. If the priest says the prayers aloud the assembly's acclamation each time is

Blessed be God for ever.

The Priest completes additional personal preparatory rites, and the people rise as he says:

Pray, brethren (brothers and sisters),

that my sacrifice and yours

may be acceptable to God,

the almighty Father.

The people reply:

May the Lord accept the sacrifice at your hands

for the praise and glory of his name,

for our good

and the good of all his holy Church.

Then the Priest says the Prayer over the Offerings, at the end of which the people acclaim:

Amen.

The Eucharistic Prayer

The Eucharistic Prayer, the center and summit of the entire celebration is a memorial proclamation of praise and thanksgiving for God's work of salvation, a proclamation in which the Body and Blood of Christ are made present by the power of the Holy Spirit and the people are joined to Christ in offering his Sacrifice to the Father.

Either of

Eucharistic Prayer 1 ("The Roman Canon")

Extending his hands, the Priest says:

The Lord be with you.

The people reply:

And with your spirit.

The Priest, raising his hands, continues:

Lift up your hearts.

The people:

We lift them up to the Lord.

The Priest, with hands extended, adds:

Let us give thanks to the Lord our God.

The people:

It is right and just.

The Priest continues with the Preface.

The renewal of all things in Christ

The following Preface is said in Masses that have no proper Preface, and for which a Preface related to a specific liturgical time is not indicated.

It is truly right and just, our duty and our salvation,

always and everywhere to give you thanks,

Lord, holy Father, almighty and eternal God,

through Christ our Lord.

In him you have been pleased to renew all things,

giving us all a share in his fullness.

For though he was in the form of God, he emptied himself

and by the blood of his Cross brought peace to all creation.

Therefore he has been exalted above all things,

and to all who obey him,

has become the source of eternal salvation.

And so, with Angels and Archangels,

with Thrones and Dominions,

and with all the hosts and Powers of heaven,

we sing the hymn of your glory,

as without end we acclaim:

The Priest concludes the Preface with the people singing or saying aloud:

Holy, Holy, Holy Lord God of hosts.

Heaven and earth are full of your glory.

Hosanna in the highest.

Blessed is he who comes in the name of the Lord.

Hosanna in the highest.

After the singing of the Sanctus the congregation kneels for the remainder of the Eucharistic Prayer.

Eucharistic Prayer 1 ("The Roman Canon")

The Priest alone recites:

To you, therefore, most merciful Father,

we make humble prayer and petition

through Jesus Christ, your Son, our Lord:

that you accept

and bless ✠ *these gifts, these offerings,*

these holy and unblemished sacrifices,

which we offer you firstly

for your holy catholic Church.

Be pleased to grant her peace,

to guard, unite and govern her

throughout the whole world,

together with your servant N. our Pope

and N. our Bishop,

and all those who, holding to the truth,

hand on the catholic and apostolic faith.

Remember, Lord, your servants (N. and N.)

and all gathered here,

whose faith and devotion are known to you.

For them, we offer you this sacrifice of praise

or they offer it for themselves

and all who are dear to them:

for the redemption of their souls,

in hope of health and well-being,

and paying their homage to you,

the eternal God, living and true.

Communicantes : Usual form

In communion with those whose memory we venerate,

especially the glorious ever-Virgin Mary,

Mother of our God and Lord, Jesus Christ,

and blessed Joseph, her Spouse,

your blessed Apostles and Martyrs,

Peter and Paul, Andrew,

(James, John,

Thomas, James, Philip,

Bartholomew, Matthew,

Simon and Jude;

Linus, Cletus, Clement, Sixtus,

Cornelius, Cyprian,

Lawrence, Chrysogonus,

John and Paul,

Cosmas and Damian)

and all your Saints;

we ask that through their merits and prayers,

in all things we may be defended

by your protecting help.

(Through Christ our Lord. Amen.)

Therefore, Lord, we pray:

graciously accept this oblation of our service,

that of your whole family;

order our days in your peace,

and command that we be delivered from eternal damnation

and counted among the flock of those you have chosen.

(Through Christ our Lord. Amen.)

Be pleased, O God, we pray,

to bless, acknowledge,

and approve this offering in every respect;

make it spiritual and acceptable,

so that it may become for us

the Body and Blood of your most beloved Son,

our Lord Jesus Christ.

On the day before he was to suffer,

he took bread in his holy and venerable hands,

and with eyes raised to heaven

to you, O God, his almighty Father,

giving you thanks, he said the blessing,

broke the bread

and gave it to his disciples, saying:

Take this, all of you, and eat of it,

for this is my Body,

which will be given up for you.

In a similar way, when supper was ended,

he took this precious chalice

in his holy and venerable hands,

and once more giving you thanks, he said the blessing

and gave the chalice to his disciples, saying:

Take this, all of you, and drink from it,

for this is the chalice of my Blood,

the Blood of the new and eternal covenant,

which will be poured out for you and for many

for the forgiveness of sins.

Do this in memory of me.

After the words of Consecration the priest says:

The mystery of faith.

The people continue, acclaiming:

Either:

We proclaim your Death, O Lord,

and profess your Resurrection

until you come again.

Or:

When we eat this Bread and drink this Cup,

we proclaim your Death, O Lord,

until you come again.

Or:

Save us, Saviour of the world,

for by your Cross and Resurrection

you have set us free.

Then the Priest alone continues:

Therefore, O Lord,

as we celebrate the memorial of the blessed Passion,

the Resurrection from the dead,

and the glorious Ascension into heaven

of Christ, your Son, our Lord,

we, your servants and your holy people,

offer to your glorious majesty

from the gifts that you have given us,

this pure victim,

this holy victim,

this spotless victim,

the holy Bread of eternal life

and the Chalice of everlasting salvation.

Be pleased to look upon these offerings

with a serene and kindly countenance,

and to accept them,

as once you were pleased to accept

the gifts of your servant Abel the just,

the sacrifice of Abraham, our father in faith,

and the offering of your high priest Melchizedek,

a holy sacrifice, a spotless victim.

In humble prayer we ask you, almighty God:

command that these gifts be borne

by the hands of your holy Angel

to your altar on high

in the sight of your divine majesty,

so that all of us, who through this participation at the altar

receive the most holy Body and Blood of your Son,

may be filled with every grace and heavenly blessing.

(Through Christ our Lord. Amen.)

Commemoration of the Dead
Remember also, Lord, your servants N. and N.,
who have gone before us with the sign of faith
and rest in the sleep of peace.
Grant them, O Lord, we pray,
and all who sleep in Christ,
a place of refreshment, light and peace.
(Through Christ our Lord. Amen.)

To us, also, your servants, who, though sinners,

hope in your abundant mercies,

graciously grant some share

and fellowship with your holy Apostles and Martyrs:

with John the Baptist, Stephen,

Matthias, Barnabas,

(Ignatius, Alexander,

Marcellinus, Peter,

Felicity, Perpetua,

Agatha, Lucy,

Agnes, Cecilia, Anastasia)

and all your Saints;

admit us, we beseech you,

into their company,

not weighing our merits,

but granting us your pardon,

through Christ our Lord.

Through whom

you continue to make all these good things, O Lord;

you sanctify them, fill them with life,

bless them, and bestow them upon us.

At the conclusion of the Eucharistic Prayer the Priest takes the
chalice and the paten with the host and, raising both, he alone
says:

Through him, and with him, and in him,

O God, almighty Father,

in the unity of the Holy Spirit,

all glory and honour is yours,

for ever and ever.

Amen.

Eucharistic Prayer I

Extending his hands, the Priest says:

The Lord be with you.

The people reply:

And with your spirit.

The Priest, raising his hands, continues:

Lift up your hearts.

The people:

We lift them up to the Lord.

The Priest, with hands extended, adds:

Let us give thanks to the Lord our God.

The people:

It is right and just.

The Priest continues with the Preface.

Eucharistic Prayer II has its own Preface, but other Prefaces can
also be used.

Preface for Eucharistic Prayer II

It is truly right and just, our duty and our salvation,

always and everywhere to give you thanks, Father most holy, through your beloved Son, Jesus Christ,

your Word through whom you made all things,

whom you sent as our Saviour and Redeemer,

incarnate by the Holy Spirit and born of the Virgin.

Fulfilling your will and gaining for you a holy people,

he stretched out his hands as he endured his Passion,

so as to break the bonds of death and manifest the resurrection.

And so, with the Angels and all the Saints

we declare your glory,

as with one voice we acclaim:

The Priest concludes the Preface with the people singing or saying aloud:

Holy, Holy, Holy Lord God of hosts.

Heaven and earth are full of your glory.

Hosanna in the highest.

Blessed is he who comes in the name of the Lord.

Hosanna in the highest.

After the singing of the Sanctus the congregation kneels for the remainder of the Eucharistic Prayer.

Eucharistic Prayer II

The Priest alone recites:

You are indeed Holy, O Lord,

the fount of all holiness.

Make holy, therefore, these gifts, we pray,

by sending down your Spirit upon them like the dewfall,

so that they may become for us

the Body and ✠ Blood of our Lord Jesus Christ.

At the time he was betrayed

and entered willingly into his Passion,

he took bread and, giving thanks, broke it,

and gave it to his disciples, saying:

Take this, all of you, and eat of it,

for this is my Body,

which will be given up for you.

In a similar way, when supper was ended,

he took the chalice

and, once more giving thanks,

he gave it to his disciples, saying:

Take this, all of you, and drink from it,

for this is the chalice of my Blood,

the Blood of the new and eternal covenant,

which will be poured out for you and for many

for the forgiveness of sins.

Do this in memory of me.

After the words of Consecration the priest says:

The mystery of faith.

The people continue, acclaiming:

Either:

We proclaim your Death, O Lord,

and profess your Resurrection

until you come again.

Or:

When we eat this Bread and drink this Cup,

we proclaim your Death, O Lord,

until you come again.

Or:

Save us, Saviour of the world,

for by your Cross and Resurrection

you have set us free.

Then the Priest alone continues:

Therefore, as we celebrate

the memorial of his Death and Resurrection,

we offer you, Lord,

the Bread of life and the Chalice of salvation,

giving thanks that you have held us worthy

to be in your presence and minister to you.

Humbly we pray

that, partaking of the Body and Blood of Christ,

we may be gathered into one by the Holy Spirit.

Remember, Lord, your Church,

spread throughout the world,

and bring her to the fullness of charity,

together with N. our Pope and N. our Bishop

and all the clergy.

In Masses for the Dead, the following may be added:
Remember your servant N.,
whom you have called (today)
from this world to yourself.
Grant that he (she) who was united with your Son in a
death like his,
may also be one with him in his Resurrection.

Remember also our brothers and sisters

who have fallen asleep in the hope of the resurrection,

and all who have died in your mercy:

welcome them into the light of your face.

Have mercy on us all, we pray,

that with the Blessed Virgin Mary, Mother of God,

with blessed Joseph, her Spouse,

with the blessed Apostles,

and all the Saints who have pleased you throughout the ages,

we may merit to be coheirs to eternal life,

and may praise and glorify you

through your Son, Jesus Christ.

At the conclusion of the Eucharistic Prayer the Priest takes the chalice and the paten with the host and, raising both, he alone says:

Through him, and with him, and in him,

O God, almighty Father,

in the unity of the Holy Spirit,

all glory and honour is yours,

for ever and ever.

Amen.

Eucharistic Prayer 111

Extending his hands, the Priest says:

The Lord be with you.

The people reply:

And with your spirit.

The Priest, raising his hands, continues:

Lift up your hearts.

The people:

We lift them up to the Lord.

The Priest, with hands extended, adds:

Let us give thanks to the Lord our God.

The people:

It is right and just.

The Priest continues with the Preface.

Common Preface 1
The renewal of all things in Christ

The following Preface is said in Masses that have no proper Preface, and for which a Preface related to a specific liturgical time is not indicated.

It is truly right and just, our duty and our salvation,

always and everywhere to give you thanks,

Lord, holy Father, almighty and eternal God,

through Christ our Lord.

In him you have been pleased to renew all things,

giving us all a share in his fullness.

For though he was in the form of God, he emptied himself

and by the blood of his Cross brought peace to all creation.

Therefore he has been exalted above all things,

and to all who obey him,

has become the source of eternal salvation.

And so, with Angels and Archangels,

with Thrones and Dominions,

and with all the hosts and Powers of heaven,

we sing the hymn of your glory,

as without end we acclaim:

The Priest concludes the Preface with the people singing or saying aloud:

Holy, Holy, Holy Lord God of hosts.

Heaven and earth are full of your glory.

Hosanna in the highest.

Blessed is he who comes in the name of the Lord.

Hosanna in the highest.

After the singing of the Sanctus the congregation kneels for the remainder of the Eucharistic Prayer.

Common Preface 11
Salvation through Christ

The following Preface is said in Masses that have no proper Preface, and for which a Preface related to a specific liturgical time is not indicated.

It is truly right and just, our duty and our salvation,

always and everywhere to give you thanks,

Lord, holy Father, almighty and eternal God.

For in goodness you created man

and, when he was justly condemned,

in mercy you redeemed him,

through Christ our Lord.

Through him the Angels praise your majesty,

Dominions adore and Powers tremble before you.

Heaven and the Virtues of heaven and the blessed Seraphim

worship together with exultation.

May our voices, we pray, join with theirs

in humble praise, as we acclaim:

The Priest concludes the Preface with the people singing or saying aloud:

Holy, Holy, Holy Lord God of hosts.

Heaven and earth are full of your glory.

Hosanna in the highest.

Blessed is he who comes in the name of the Lord.

Hosanna in the highest.

After the singing of the Sanctus the congregation kneels for the remainder of the Eucharistic Prayer.

Common Preface 111

Praise to God for the creation and restoration of the human race

The following Preface is said in Masses that have no proper Preface, and for which a Preface related to a specific liturgical time is not indicated.

It is truly right and just, our duty and our salvation,

always and everywhere to give you thanks,

Lord, holy Father, almighty and eternal God.

For just as through your beloved Son

you created the human race,

so also through him

with great goodness you formed it anew.

And so, it is right that all your creatures serve you,

all the redeemed praise you,

and all your Saints with one heart bless you.

Therefore, we, too, extol you with all the Angels,

as in joyful celebration we acclaim:

The Priest concludes the Preface with the people singing or saying aloud:

Holy, Holy, Holy Lord God of hosts.

Heaven and earth are full of your glory.

Hosanna in the highest.

Blessed is he who comes in the name of the Lord.

Hosanna in the highest.

After the singing of the Sanctus the congregation kneels for the remainder of the Eucharistic Prayer.

Common Preface IV

Praise, the gift of God

The following Preface is said in Masses that have no proper Preface, and for which a Preface related to a specific liturgical time is not indicated.

It is truly right and just, our duty and our salvation,

always and everywhere to give you thanks,

Lord, holy Father, almighty and eternal God.

For, although you have no need of our praise,

yet our thanksgiving is itself your gift,

since our praises add nothing to your greatness

but profit us for salvation,

through Christ our Lord.

And so, in company with the choirs of Angels,

we praise you, and with joy we proclaim:

The Priest concludes the Preface with the people singing or saying aloud:

Holy, Holy, Holy Lord God of hosts.

Heaven and earth are full of your glory.

Hosanna in the highest.

Blessed is he who comes in the name of the Lord.

Hosanna in the highest.

After the singing of the Sanctus the congregation kneels for the remainder of the Eucharistic Prayer.

Common Preface V
The proclamation of the Mystery of Christ

The following Preface is said in Masses that have no proper Preface, and for which a Preface related to a specific liturgical time is not indicated.

It is truly right and just, our duty and our salvation,

always and everywhere to give you thanks,

Lord, holy Father, almighty and eternal God,

through Christ our Lord.

His Death we celebrate in love,

his Resurrection we confess with living faith,

and his Coming in glory we await with unwavering hope.

And so, with all the Angels and Saints,

we praise you, as without end we acclaim:

The Priest concludes the Preface with the people singing or saying aloud:

Holy, Holy, Holy Lord God of hosts.

Heaven and earth are full of your glory.

Hosanna in the highest.

Blessed is he who comes in the name of the Lord.

Hosanna in the highest.

After the singing of the Sanctus the congregation kneels for the remainder of the Eucharistic Prayer.

Common Preface VI

The mystery of salvation in Christ

The following Preface is said in Masses that have no proper Preface, and for which a Preface related to a specific liturgical time is not indicated.

It is truly right and just, our duty and our salvation,

always and everywhere to give you thanks, Father most holy,

through your beloved Son, Jesus Christ,

your Word through whom you made all things,

whom you sent as our Saviour and Redeemer,

incarnate by the Holy Spirit and born of the Virgin.

Fulfilling your will and gaining for you a holy people,

he stretched out his hands as he endured his Passion,

so as to break the bonds of death and manifest the resurrection.

And so, with the Angels and all the Saints,

we declare your glory,

as with one voice we acclaim:

The Priest concludes the Preface with the people singing or saying aloud:

Holy, Holy, Holy Lord God of hosts.

Heaven and earth are full of your glory.

Hosanna in the highest.

Blessed is he who comes in the name of the Lord.

Hosanna in the highest.

After the singing of the Sanctus the congregation kneels for the remainder of the Eucharistic Prayer.

Preface I for the Dead

The hope of resurrection in Christ

The following Preface is said in Masses for the Dead.

It is truly right and just, our duty and our salvation,

always and everywhere to give you thanks,

Lord, holy Father, almighty and eternal God,

through Christ our Lord.

In him the hope of blessed resurrection has dawned,

that those saddened by the certainty of dying

might be consoled by the promise of immortality to come.

Indeed for your faithful, Lord,

life is changed not ended,

and, when this earthly dwelling turns to dust,

an eternal dwelling is made ready for them in heaven.

And so, with Angels and Archangels,

with Thrones and Dominions,

and with all the hosts and Powers of heaven,

we sing the hymn of your glory,

as without end we acclaim:

The Priest concludes the Preface with the people singing or saying aloud:

Holy, Holy, Holy Lord God of hosts.

Heaven and earth are full of your glory.

Hosanna in the highest.

Blessed is he who comes in the name of the Lord.

Hosanna in the highest.

After the singing of the Sanctus the congregation kneels for the remainder of the Eucharistic Prayer.

Preface II for the Dead

Christ died so that we might live

The following Preface is said in Masses for the Dead.

It is truly right and just, our duty and our salvation,

always and everywhere to give you thanks,

Lord, holy Father, almighty and eternal God,

through Christ our Lord.

For as one alone he accepted death,

so that we might all escape from dying;

as one man he chose to die,

so that in your sight we all might live for ever.

And so, in company with the choirs of Angels,

we praise you, and with joy we proclaim:

The Priest concludes the Preface with the people singing or saying aloud:

Holy, Holy, Holy Lord God of hosts.

Heaven and earth are full of your glory.

Hosanna in the highest.

Blessed is he who comes in the name of the Lord.

Hosanna in the highest.

After the singing of the Sanctus the congregation kneels for the remainder of the Eucharistic Prayer.

Preface III for the Dead

Christ, the salvation and the life

The following Preface is said in Masses for the Dead.

It is truly right and just, our duty and our salvation,

always and everywhere to give you thanks,

Lord, holy Father, almighty and eternal God,

through Christ our Lord.

For he is the salvation of the world,

the life of the human race,

the resurrection of the dead.

Through him the host of Angels adores your majesty

and rejoices in your presence for ever.

May our voices, we pray, join with theirs

in one chorus of exultant praise, as we acclaim:

The Priest concludes the Preface with the people singing or saying aloud:

Holy, Holy, Holy Lord God of hosts.

Heaven and earth are full of your glory.

Hosanna in the highest.

Blessed is he who comes in the name of the Lord.

Hosanna in the highest.

After the singing of the Sanctus the congregation kneels for the remainder of the Eucharistic Prayer.

Preface IV for the Dead

From earthly life to heavenly glory

The following Preface is said in Masses for the Dead.

It is truly right and just, our duty and our salvation,

always and everywhere to give you thanks,

Lord, holy Father, almighty and eternal God.

For it is at your summons that we come to birth,

by your will that we are governed,

and at your command that we return,

on account of sin,

to the earth from which we came.

And when you give the sign,

44

we who have been redeemed by the Death of your Son,

shall be raised up to the glory of his Resurrection.

And so, with the company of Angels and Saints,

we sing the hymn of your praise,

as without end we acclaim:

The Priest concludes the Preface with the people singing or saying aloud:

Holy, Holy, Holy Lord God of hosts.

Heaven and earth are full of your glory.

Hosanna in the highest.

Blessed is he who comes in the name of the Lord.

Hosanna in the highest.

After the singing of the Sanctus the congregation kneels for the remainder of the Eucharistic Prayer.

Preface V for the Dead

Our resurrection through the victory of Christ

The following Preface is said in Masses for the Dead.

It is truly right and just, our duty and our salvation,

always and everywhere to give you thanks,

Lord, holy Father, almighty and eternal God.

For even though by our own fault we perish,

yet by your compassion and your grace,

when seized by death according to our sins,

we are redeemed through Christ's great victory,

and with him called back into life.

And so, with the Powers of heaven,

we worship you constantly on earth,

and before your majesty

without end we acclaim:

The Priest concludes the Preface with the people singing or saying aloud:

Holy, Holy, Holy Lord God of hosts.

Heaven and earth are full of your glory.

Hosanna in the highest.

Blessed is he who comes in the name of the Lord.

Hosanna in the highest.

After the singing of the Sanctus the congregation kneels for the remainder of the Eucharistic Prayer.

Preface of Holy Pastors

The presence of holy Pastors in the Church

The following Preface is said on the Solemnities and Feasts of Holy Pastors. It may also be said on their Memorials.

It is truly right and just, our duty and our salvation,

always and everywhere to give you thanks,

Lord, holy Father, almighty and eternal God,

through Christ our Lord.

For, as on the festival of Saint N. you bid your Church rejoice,

so, too, you strengthen her by the example of his holy life,

teach her by his words of preaching,

and keep her safe in answer to his prayers.

And so, with the company of Angels and Saints,

we sing the hymn of your praise,

as without end we acclaim:

The Priest concludes the Preface with the people singing or saying aloud:

Holy, Holy, Holy Lord God of hosts.

Heaven and earth are full of your glory.

Hosanna in the highest.

Blessed is he who comes in the name of the Lord.

Hosanna in the highest.

After the singing of the Sanctus the congregation kneels for the remainder of the Eucharistic Prayer.

Preface of 1 Holy Martyrs
The sign and example of martyrdom

The following Preface is said on the Solemnities and Feasts of Holy Martyrs. It may also be said on their Memorials.

It is truly right and just, our duty and our salvation,

always and everywhere to give you thanks,

Lord, holy Father, almighty and eternal God.

For the blood of your blessed Martyr N.,

poured out like Christ's to glorify your name,

shows forth your marvellous works,

by which in our weakness you perfect your power

and on the feeble bestow strength to bear you witness,

through Christ our Lord.

And so, with the Powers of heaven,

we worship you constantly on earth,

and before your majesty

without end we acclaim:

The Priest concludes the Preface with the people singing or saying aloud:

Holy, Holy, Holy Lord God of hosts.

Heaven and earth are full of your glory.

Hosanna in the highest.

Blessed is he who comes in the name of the Lord.

Hosanna in the highest.

After the singing of the Sanctus the congregation kneels for the remainder of the Eucharistic Prayer.

Preface I of Apostles

The Apostles, shepherds of God's people

The following Preface is said in Masses of the Apostles, especially of Saints Peter and Paul.

It is truly right and just, our duty and our salvation,

always and everywhere to give you thanks,

Lord, holy Father, almighty and eternal God.

For you, eternal Shepherd, do not desert your flock,

but through the blessed Apostles

watch over it and protect it always,

so that it may be governed

by those you have appointed shepherds

to lead it in the name of your Son.

And so, with Angels and Archangels,

with Thrones and Dominions,

and with all the hosts and Powers of heaven,

we sing the hymn of your glory,

as without end we acclaim:

The Priest concludes the Preface with the people singing or saying aloud:

Holy, Holy, Holy Lord God of hosts.

Heaven and earth are full of your glory.

Hosanna in the highest.

Blessed is he who comes in the name of the Lord.

Hosanna in the highest.

After the singing of the Sanctus the congregation kneels for the remainder of the Eucharistic Prayer.

Preface II of Apostles
The apostolic foundation and witness

The following Preface is said in Masses of the Apostles and Evangelists.

It is truly right and just, our duty and our salvation,

always and everywhere to give you thanks,

Lord, holy Father, almighty and eternal God,

through Christ our Lord.

For you have built your Church

to stand firm on apostolic foundations,

to be a lasting sign of your holiness on earth

and offer all humanity your heavenly teaching.

Therefore, now and for ages unending,

with all the host of Angels,

we sing to you with all our hearts,

crying out as we acclaim:

The Priest concludes the Preface with the people singing or saying aloud:

Holy, Holy, Holy Lord God of hosts.

Heaven and earth are full of your glory.

Hosanna in the highest.

Blessed is he who comes in the name of the Lord.

Hosanna in the highest.

After the singing of the Sanctus the congregation kneels for the remainder of the Eucharistic Prayer.

Preface I of the Most Holy Eucharist
The Sacrifice and the Sacrament of Christ

The following Preface is said in the Mass of the Lord's Supper. It may also be said on the Solemnity of the Most Holy Body and Blood of Christ and in Votive Masses of the Most Holy Eucharist.

It is truly right and just, our duty and our salvation,

always and everywhere to give you thanks,

Lord, holy Father, almighty and eternal God,

through Christ our Lord.

For he is the true and eternal Priest,

who instituted the pattern of an everlasting sacrifice

and was the first to offer himself as the saving Victim,

commanding us to make this offering as his memorial.

As we eat his flesh that was sacrificed for us,

we are made strong,

and, as we drink his Blood that was poured out for us,

we are washed clean.

And so, with Angels and Archangels,

with Thrones and Dominions,

and with all the hosts and Powers of heaven,

we sing the hymn of your glory,

as without end we acclaim:

The Priest concludes the Preface with the people singing or saying aloud:

Holy, Holy, Holy Lord God of hosts.

Heaven and earth are full of your glory.

Hosanna in the highest.

Blessed is he who comes in the name of the Lord.

Hosanna in the highest.

After the singing of the Sanctus the congregation kneels for the remainder of the Eucharistic Prayer.

Preface II of the Most Holy Eucharist
The fruits of the Most Holy Eucharist

The following Preface is said on the Solemnity of the Most Holy Body and Blood of Christ (Corpus Christi) and in Votive Masses of the Most Holy Eucharist.

It is truly right and just, our duty and our salvation,

always and everywhere to give you thanks,

Lord, holy Father, almighty and eternal God,

through Christ our Lord.

For at the Last Supper with his Apostles,

establishing for the ages to come the saving memorial of the Cross,

he offered himself to you as the unblemished Lamb,

the acceptable gift of perfect praise.

Nourishing your faithful by this sacred mystery,

you make them holy, so that the human race,

bounded by one world,

may be enlightened by one faith

and united by one bond of charity.

And so, we approach the table of this wondrous Sacrament,

so that, bathed in the sweetness of your grace,

we may pass over to the heavenly realities here foreshadowed.

Therefore, all creatures of heaven and earth

sing a new song in adoration,

and we, with all the host of Angels,

cry out, and without end we acclaim:

The Priest concludes the Preface with the people singing or saying aloud:

Holy, Holy, Holy Lord God of hosts.

Heaven and earth are full of your glory.

Hosanna in the highest.

Blessed is he who comes in the name of the Lord.

Hosanna in the highest.

After the singing of the Sanctus the congregation kneels for the remainder of the Eucharistic Prayer.

Preface I of the Blessed Virgin Mary

The Motherhood of the Blessed Virgin Mary

The following Preface is said in Masses of the Blessed Virgin Mary, with the mention at the appropriate place of the particular celebration, as indicated in the individual Masses.

It is truly right and just, our duty and our salvation,

always and everywhere to give you thanks,

Lord, holy Father, almighty and eternal God,

and to praise, bless, and glorify your name

(on the Solemnity of the Motherhood / on the feast day / on the Nativity / in veneration)

of the Blessed ever-Virgin Mary.

For by the overshadowing of the Holy Spirit

she conceived your Only Begotten Son,

and without losing the glory of virginity,

brought forth into the world the eternal Light,

Jesus Christ our Lord.

Through him the Angels praise your majesty,

Dominions adore and Powers tremble before you.

Heaven and the Virtues of heaven and the blessed Seraphim

worship together with exultation.

May our voices, we pray, join with theirs

in humble praise, as we acclaim:

The Priest concludes the Preface with the people singing or saying aloud:

Holy, Holy, Holy Lord God of hosts.

Heaven and earth are full of your glory.

Hosanna in the highest.

Blessed is he who comes in the name of the Lord.

Hosanna in the highest.

After the singing of the Sanctus the congregation kneels for the remainder of the Eucharistic Prayer.

Preface II of the Blessed Virgin Mary

The Church praises God with the words of Mary

The following Preface is said in Masses of the Blessed Virgin Mary.

It is truly right and just, our duty and our salvation,

to praise your mighty deeds in the exaltation of all the Saints,

and especially, as we celebrate the memory of the Blessed Virgin Mary,

to proclaim your kindness as we echo her thankful hymn of praise.

For truly even to earth's ends you have done great things

and extended your abundant mercy from age to age:

when you looked on the lowliness of your handmaid,

you gave us through her the author of our salvation,

your Son, Jesus Christ, our Lord.

Through him the host of Angels adores your majesty

and rejoices in your presence for ever.

May our voices, we pray, join with theirs

in one chorus of exultant praise, as we acclaim:

The Priest concludes the Preface with the people singing or saying aloud:

Holy, Holy, Holy Lord God of hosts.

Heaven and earth are full of your glory.

Hosanna in the highest.

Blessed is he who comes in the name of the Lord.

Hosanna in the highest.

After the singing of the Sanctus the congregation kneels for the remainder of the Eucharistic Prayer.

Preface I of the Most Holy Eucharist
The Sacrifice and the Sacrament of Christ

The following Preface is said in the Mass of the Lord's Supper. It may also be said on the Solemnity of the Most Holy Body and Blood of Christ and in Votive Masses of the Most Holy Eucharist.

It is truly right and just, our duty and our salvation,

always and everywhere to give you thanks,

Lord, holy Father, almighty and eternal God,

through Christ our Lord.

For he is the true and eternal Priest,

who instituted the pattern of an everlasting sacrifice

and was the first to offer himself as the saving Victim,

commanding us to make this offering as his memorial.

As we eat his flesh that was sacrificed for us,

we are made strong,

and, as we drink his Blood that was poured out for us,

we are washed clean.

And so, with Angels and Archangels,

with Thrones and Dominions,

and with all the hosts and Powers of heaven,

we sing the hymn of your glory,

as without end we acclaim:

The Priest concludes the Preface with the people singing or saying aloud:

Holy, Holy, Holy Lord God of hosts.

Heaven and earth are full of your glory.

Hosanna in the highest.

Blessed is he who comes in the name of the Lord.

Hosanna in the highest.

After the singing of the Sanctus the congregation kneels for the remainder of the Eucharistic Prayer.

Preface I1 of the Most Holy Eucharist
The fruits of the Most Holy Eucharist

The following Preface is said on the Solemnity of the Most Holy Body and Blood of Christ (Corpus Christi) and in Votive Masses of the Most Holy Eucharist.

It is truly right and just, our duty and our salvation,

always and everywhere to give you thanks,

Lord, holy Father, almighty and eternal God,

through Christ our Lord.

For at the Last Supper with his Apostles,

establishing for the ages to come the saving memorial of the
Cross,

he offered himself to you as the unblemished Lamb,

the acceptable gift of perfect praise.

Nourishing your faithful by this sacred mystery,

you make them holy, so that the human race,

bounded by one world,

may be enlightened by one faith

and united by one bond of charity.

And so, we approach the table of this wondrous Sacrament,

so that, bathed in the sweetness of your grace,

we may pass over to the heavenly realities here foreshadowed.

Therefore, all creatures of heaven and earth

sing a new song in adoration,

and we, with all the host of Angels,

cry out, and without end we acclaim:

The Priest concludes the Preface with the people singing or saying aloud:

Holy, Holy, Holy Lord God of hosts.

Heaven and earth are full of your glory.

Hosanna in the highest.

Blessed is he who comes in the name of the Lord.

Hosanna in the highest.

After the singing of the Sanctus the congregation kneels for the remainder of the Eucharistic Prayer.

Preface I of the Ascension of the Lord
The mystery of the Ascension

The following Preface is said on the day of the Ascension of the Lord. It may be said on the days between the Ascension and Pentecost in all Masses that have no proper Preface.

It is truly right and just, our duty and our salvation,

always and everywhere to give you thanks,

Lord, holy Father, almighty and eternal God.

For the Lord Jesus, the King of glory,

conqueror of sin and death,

ascended (today) to the highest heavens,

as the Angels gazed in wonder.

Mediator between God and man,

judge of the world and Lord of hosts,

he ascended, not to distance himself from our lowly state

but that we, his members, might be confident of following

where he, our Head and Founder, has gone before.

Therefore, overcome with paschal joy,

every land, every people exults in your praise

and even the heavenly Powers, with the angelic hosts,

sing together the unending hymn of your glory,

as they acclaim:

The Priest concludes the Preface with the people singing or saying aloud:

Holy, Holy, Holy Lord God of hosts.

Heaven and earth are full of your glory.

Hosanna in the highest.

Blessed is he who comes in the name of the Lord.

Hosanna in the highest.

After the singing of the Sanctus the congregation kneels for the remainder of the Eucharistic Prayer.

Preface II of the Ascension of the Lord
The mystery of the Ascension

The following Preface is said on the day of the Ascension of the Lord. It may be said on the days between the Ascension and Pentecost in all Masses that have no proper Preface.

It is truly right and just, our duty and our salvation,

always and everywhere to give you thanks,

Lord, holy Father, almighty and eternal God,

through Christ our Lord.

For after his Resurrection

he plainly appeared to all his disciples

and was taken up to heaven in their sight,

that he might make us sharers in his divinity.

Therefore, overcome with paschal joy,

every land, every people exults in your praise

and even the heavenly Powers, with the angelic hosts,

sing together the unending hymn of your glory,

as they acclaim:

The Priest concludes the Preface with the people singing or
saying aloud:

Holy, Holy, Holy Lord God of hosts.

Heaven and earth are full of your glory.

Hosanna in the highest.

Blessed is he who comes in the name of the Lord.

Hosanna in the highest.

After the singing of the Sanctus the congregation kneels for the
remainder of the Eucharistic Prayer.

Preface I of the Sundays in Ordinary Time
The Paschal Mystery and the People of God

The following Preface is said on Sundays in Ordinary Time.

It is truly right and just, our duty and our salvation,

always and everywhere to give you thanks,

Lord, holy Father, almighty and eternal God,

through Christ our Lord.

For through his Paschal Mystery,

he accomplished the marvellous deed,

by which he has freed us from the yoke of sin and death,

summoning us to the glory of being now called

a chosen race, a royal priesthood,

a holy nation, a people for your own possession,

to proclaim everywhere your mighty works,

for you have called us out of darkness

into your own wonderful light.

And so, with Angels and Archangels,

with Thrones and Dominions,

and with all the hosts and Powers of heaven,

we sing the hymn of your glory,

as without end we acclaim:

The Priest concludes the Preface with the people singing or saying aloud:

Holy, Holy, Holy Lord God of hosts.

Heaven and earth are full of your glory.

Hosanna in the highest.

Blessed is he who comes in the name of the Lord.

Hosanna in the highest.

After the singing of the Sanctus the congregation kneels for the remainder of the Eucharistic Prayer.

Preface II of the Sundays in Ordinary Time

The mystery of salvation

The following Preface is said on Sundays in Ordinary Time.

It is truly right and just, our duty and our salvation,

always and everywhere to give you thanks,

Lord, holy Father, almighty and eternal God,

through Christ our Lord.

For out of compassion for the waywardness that is ours,

he humbled himself and was born of the Virgin;

by the passion of the Cross he freed us from unending death,

and by rising from the dead he gave us life eternal.

And so, with Angels and Archangels,

with Thrones and Dominions,

and with all the hosts and Powers of heaven,

we sing the hymn of your glory,

as without end we acclaim:

The Priest concludes the Preface with the people singing or saying aloud:

Holy, Holy, Holy Lord God of hosts.

Heaven and earth are full of your glory.

Hosanna in the highest.

Blessed is he who comes in the name of the Lord.

Hosanna in the highest.

After the singing of the Sanctus the congregation kneels for the remainder of the Eucharistic Prayer.

Preface III of the Sundays in Ordinary Time
The salvation of man by a man

The following Preface is said on Sundays in Ordinary Time.

It is truly right and just, our duty and our salvation,

always and everywhere to give you thanks,

Lord, holy Father, almighty and eternal God.

For we know it belongs to your boundless glory,

that you came to the aid of mortal beings with your divinity

and even fashioned for us a remedy out of mortality itself,

that the cause of our downfall

might become the means of our salvation,

through Christ our Lord.

Through him the host of Angels adores your majesty

and rejoices in your presence for ever.

May our voices, we pray, join with theirs

in one chorus of exultant praise, as we acclaim:

The Priest concludes the Preface with the people singing or saying aloud:

Holy, Holy, Holy Lord God of hosts.

Heaven and earth are full of your glory.

Hosanna in the highest.

Blessed is he who comes in the name of the Lord.

Hosanna in the highest.

After the singing of the Sanctus the congregation kneels for the remainder of the Eucharistic Prayer.

The history of salvation

The following Preface is said on Sundays in Ordinary Time.

It is truly right and just, our duty and our salvation,

always and everywhere to give you thanks,

Lord, holy Father, almighty and eternal God,

through Christ our Lord.

For by his birth he brought renewal

to humanity's fallen state,

and by his suffering, cancelled out our sins;

by his rising from the dead

he has opened the way to eternal life,

and by ascending to you, O Father,

he has unlocked the gates of heaven.

And so, with the company of Angels and Saints,

we sing the hymn of your praise,

as without end we acclaim:

The Priest concludes the Preface with the people singing or saying aloud:

Holy, Holy, Holy Lord God of hosts.

Heaven and earth are full of your glory.

Hosanna in the highest.

Blessed is he who comes in the name of the Lord.

Hosanna in the highest.

After the singing of the Sanctus the congregation kneels for the remainder of the Eucharistic Prayer.

Preface V of the Sundays in Ordinary Time

Creation

The following Preface is said on Sundays in Ordinary Time.

It is truly right and just, our duty and our salvation,

always and everywhere to give you thanks,

Lord, holy Father, almighty and eternal God.

For you laid the foundations of the world

and have arranged the changing of times and seasons;

you formed man in your own image

and set humanity over the whole world in all its wonder,

to rule in your name over all you have made

and for ever praise you in your mighty works,

through Christ our Lord.

And so, with all the Angels, we praise you,

as in joyful celebration we acclaim:

The Priest concludes the Preface with the people singing or saying aloud:

Holy, Holy, Holy Lord God of hosts.

Heaven and earth are full of your glory.

Hosanna in the highest.

Blessed is he who comes in the name of the Lord.

Hosanna in the highest.

After the singing of the Sanctus the congregation kneels for the remainder of the Eucharistic Prayer.

Preface VI of the Sundays in Ordinary Time

The pledge of the eternal Passover

The following Preface is said on Sundays in Ordinary Time.

It is truly right and just, our duty and our salvation,

always and everywhere to give you thanks,

Lord, holy Father, almighty and eternal God.

For in you we live and move and have our being,

and while in this body

we not only experience the daily effects of your care,

but even now possess the pledge of life eternal.

For, having received the first fruits of the Spirit,

through whom you raised up Jesus from the dead,

we hope for an everlasting share in the Paschal Mystery.

And so, with all the Angels, we praise you,

as in joyful celebration we acclaim:

The Priest concludes the Preface with the people singing or saying aloud:

Holy, Holy, Holy Lord God of hosts.

Heaven and earth are full of your glory.

Hosanna in the highest.

73

Blessed is he who comes in the name of the Lord.

Hosanna in the highest.

After the singing of the Sanctus the congregation kneels for the remainder of the Eucharistic Prayer.

Preface VII of the Sundays in Ordinary Time

Salvation through the obedience of Christ

The following Preface is said on Sundays in Ordinary Time.

It is truly right and just, our duty and our salvation,

always and everywhere to give you thanks,

Lord, holy Father, almighty and eternal God.

For you so loved the world

that in your mercy you sent us the Redeemer,

to live like us in all things but sin,

so that you might love in us what you loved in your Son,

by whose obedience we have been restored to those gifts of yours

that, by sinning, we had lost in disobedience.

And so, Lord, with all the Angels and Saints,

we, too, give you thanks, as in exultation we acclaim:

The Priest concludes the Preface with the people singing or saying aloud:

Holy, Holy, Holy Lord God of hosts.

Heaven and earth are full of your glory.

Hosanna in the highest.

Blessed is he who comes in the name of the Lord.

Hosanna in the highest.

After the singing of the Sanctus the congregation kneels for the remainder of the Eucharistic Prayer.

Preface VIII of the Sundays in Ordinary Time

The Church united by the unity of the Trinity

The following Preface is said on Sundays in Ordinary Time.

It is truly right and just, our duty and our salvation,

always and everywhere to give you thanks,

Lord, holy Father, almighty and eternal God.

For, when your children were scattered afar by sin,

through the Blood of your Son and the power of the Spirit, you gathered them again to yourself,

that a people, formed as one by the unity of the Trinity,

made the body of Christ and the temple of the Holy Spirit,

might, to the praise of your manifold wisdom,

be manifest as the Church.

And so, in company with the choirs of Angels,

we praise you, and with joy we proclaim:

The Priest concludes the Preface with the people singing or saying aloud:

Holy, Holy, Holy Lord God of hosts.

Heaven and earth are full of your glory.

Hosanna in the highest.

Blessed is he who comes in the name of the Lord.

Hosanna in the highest.

After the singing of the Sanctus the congregation kneels for the remainder of the Eucharistic Prayer.

Preface I of the Passion of the Lord

The power of the Cross

The following Preface is said during the Fifth Week of Lent and in Masses of the mysteries of the Cross and Passion of the Lord.

It is truly right and just, our duty and our salvation,

always and everywhere to give you thanks,

Lord, holy Father, almighty and eternal God.

For through the saving Passion of your Son

the whole world has received a heart

to confess the infinite power of your majesty,

since by the wondrous power of the Cross

your judgement on the world is now revealed

and the authority of Christ crucified.

And so, Lord, with all the Angels and Saints,

we, too, give you thanks, as in exultation we acclaim:

The Priest concludes the Preface with the people singing or saying aloud:

Holy, Holy, Holy Lord God of hosts.

Heaven and earth are full of your glory.

Hosanna in the highest.

Blessed is he who comes in the name of the Lord.

Hosanna in the highest.

After the singing of the Sanctus the congregation kneels for the remainder of the Eucharistic Prayer.

Preface II of the Passion of the Lord
The victory of the Passion

The following Preface is said on Monday, Tuesday, and Wednesday of Holy Week.

It is truly right and just, our duty and our salvation,

always and everywhere to give you thanks,

Lord, holy Father, almighty and eternal God,

through Christ our Lord.

For the days of his saving Passion

and glorious Resurrection are approaching,

by which the pride of the ancient foe is vanquished

and the mystery of our redemption in Christ is celebrated.

Through him the host of Angels adores your majesty

and rejoices in your presence for ever.

May our voices, we pray, join with theirs

in one chorus of exultant praise, as we acclaim:

The Priest concludes the Preface with the people singing or
saying aloud:

Holy, Holy, Holy Lord God of hosts.

Heaven and earth are full of your glory.

Hosanna in the highest.

Blessed is he who comes in the name of the Lord.

Hosanna in the highest.

After the singing of the Sanctus the congregation kneels for the
remainder of the Eucharistic Prayer.

Preface I of Easter
The Paschal Mystery

The following Preface is said during Easter Time. At the Easter
Vigil, is said on this night; on Easter Sunday and throughout the
Octave of Easter, is said on this day; on other days of Easter
Time, is said in this time.

It is truly right and just, our duty and our salvation,

at all times to acclaim you, O Lord,

but (on this night / on this day / in this time) above all

to laud you yet more gloriously,

when Christ our Passover has been sacrificed.

For he is the true Lamb

who has taken away the sins of the world;

by dying he has destroyed our death,

and by rising, restored our life.

Therefore, overcome with paschal joy,

every land, every people exults in your praise

and even the heavenly Powers, with the angelic hosts,

sing together the unending hymn of your glory,

as they acclaim:

The Priest concludes the Preface with the people singing or saying aloud:

Holy, Holy, Holy Lord God of hosts.

Heaven and earth are full of your glory.

Hosanna in the highest.

Blessed is he who comes in the name of the Lord.

Hosanna in the highest.

After the singing of the Sanctus the congregation kneels for the remainder of the Eucharistic Prayer.

Preface II of Easter
New life in Christ

The following Preface is said during Easter Time.

It is truly right and just, our duty and our salvation,

at all times to acclaim you, O Lord,

but in this time above all to laud you yet more gloriously,

when Christ our Passover has been sacrificed.

Through him the children of light rise to eternal life

and the halls of the heavenly Kingdom

are thrown open to the faithful;

for his Death is our ransom from death,

and in his rising the life of all has risen.

Therefore, overcome with paschal joy,

every land, every people exults in your praise

and even the heavenly Powers, with the angelic hosts,

sing together the unending hymn of your glory,

as they acclaim:

The Priest concludes the Preface with the people singing or saying aloud:

Holy, Holy, Holy Lord God of hosts.

Heaven and earth are full of your glory.

Hosanna in the highest.

Blessed is he who comes in the name of the Lord.

Hosanna in the highest.

After the singing of the Sanctus the congregation kneels for the remainder of the Eucharistic Prayer.

Preface III of Easter

Christ living and always interceding for us

The following Preface is said during Easter Time.

It is truly right and just, our duty and our salvation,

at all times to acclaim you, O Lord,

but in this time above all to laud you yet more gloriously,

when Christ our Passover has been sacrificed.

He never ceases to offer himself for us

but defends us and ever pleads our cause before you:

he is the sacrificial Victim who dies no more,

the Lamb, once slain, who lives for ever.

Therefore, overcome with paschal joy,

every land, every people exults in your praise

and even the heavenly Powers, with the angelic hosts,

sing together the unending hymn of your glory,

as they acclaim:

The Priest concludes the Preface with the people singing or saying aloud:

Holy, Holy, Holy Lord God of hosts.

Heaven and earth are full of your glory.

Hosanna in the highest.

Blessed is he who comes in the name of the Lord.

Hosanna in the highest.

After the singing of the Sanctus the congregation kneels for the remainder of the Eucharistic Prayer.

The restoration of the universe through the Paschal Mystery

The following Preface is said during Easter Time.

It is truly right and just, our duty and our salvation,

at all times to acclaim you, O Lord,

but in this time above all to laud you yet more gloriously,

when Christ our Passover has been sacrificed.

For, with the old order destroyed,

a universe cast down is renewed,

and integrity of life is restored to us in Christ.

Therefore, overcome with paschal joy,

every land, every people exults in your praise

and even the heavenly Powers, with the angelic hosts,

sing together the unending hymn of your glory,

as they acclaim:

The Priest concludes the Preface with the people singing or saying aloud:

Holy, Holy, Holy Lord God of hosts.

Heaven and earth are full of your glory.

Hosanna in the highest.

Blessed is he who comes in the name of the Lord.

Hosanna in the highest.

After the singing of the Sanctus the congregation kneels for the remainder of the Eucharistic Prayer.

Preface V of Easter
Christ, Priest and Victim

The following Preface is said during Easter Time.

It is truly right and just, our duty and our salvation,

at all times to acclaim you, O Lord,

but in this time above all to laud you yet more gloriously,

when Christ our Passover has been sacrificed.

By the oblation of his Body,

he brought the sacrifices of old to fulfilment

in the reality of the Cross

and, by commending himself to you for our salvation,

showed himself the Priest, the Altar, and the Lamb of sacrifice.

Therefore, overcome with paschal joy,

every land, every people exults in your praise

and even the heavenly Powers, with the angelic hosts,

sing together the unending hymn of your glory,

as they acclaim:

The Priest concludes the Preface with the people singing or saying aloud:

Holy, Holy, Holy Lord God of hosts.

Heaven and earth are full of your glory.

Hosanna in the highest.

Blessed is he who comes in the name of the Lord.

Hosanna in the highest.

After the singing of the Sanctus the congregation kneels for the remainder of the Eucharistic Prayer.

Preface I of Lent
The spiritual meaning of Lent

The following Preface is said in Masses of Lent, especially on Sundays when a more specific Preface is not prescribed.

It is truly right and just, our duty and our salvation,

always and everywhere to give you thanks,

Lord, holy Father, almighty and eternal God,

through Christ our Lord.

For by your gracious gift each year

your faithful await the sacred paschal feasts

with the joy of minds made pure,

so that, more eagerly intent on prayer

and on the works of charity,

and participating in the mysteries

by which they have been reborn,

they may be led to the fullness of grace

that you bestow on your sons and daughters.

And so, with Angels and Archangels,

with Thrones and Dominions,

and with all the hosts and Powers of heaven,

we sing the hymn of your glory,

as without end we acclaim:

The Priest concludes the Preface with the people singing or saying aloud:

Holy, Holy, Holy Lord God of hosts.

Heaven and earth are full of your glory.

Hosanna in the highest.

Blessed is he who comes in the name of the Lord.

Hosanna in the highest.

After the singing of the Sanctus the congregation kneels for the remainder of the Eucharistic Prayer.

Preface II of Lent

Spiritual penance

The following Preface is said in Masses of Lent, especially on Sundays when a more specific Preface is not prescribed.

It is truly right and just, our duty and our salvation,

always and everywhere to give you thanks,

Lord, holy Father, almighty and eternal God.

For you have given your children a sacred time

for the renewing and purifying of their hearts,

that, freed from disordered affections,

they may so deal with the things of this passing world

as to hold rather to the things that eternally endure.

And so, with all the Angels and Saints,

we praise you, as without end we acclaim:

The Priest concludes the Preface with the people singing or saying aloud:

Holy, Holy, Holy Lord God of hosts.

Heaven and earth are full of your glory.

Hosanna in the highest.

Blessed is he who comes in the name of the Lord.

Hosanna in the highest.

After the singing of the Sanctus the congregation kneels for the remainder of the Eucharistic Prayer.

Preface III of Lent

The fruits of abstinence

The following Preface is said in Masses of the weekdays of Lent and on days of fasting.

It is truly right and just, our duty and our salvation,

always and everywhere to give you thanks,

Lord, holy Father, almighty and eternal God.

For you will that our self-denial should give you thanks,

humble our sinful pride,

contribute to the feeding of the poor,

and so help us imitate you in your kindness.

And so we glorify you with countless Angels,

as with one voice of praise we acclaim:

The Priest concludes the Preface with the people singing or saying aloud:

Holy, Holy, Holy Lord God of hosts.

Heaven and earth are full of your glory.

Hosanna in the highest.

Blessed is he who comes in the name of the Lord.

Hosanna in the highest.

After the singing of the Sanctus the congregation kneels for the remainder of the Eucharistic Prayer.

Preface IV of Lent

The fruits of fasting

The following Preface is said in Masses of the weekdays of Lent and on days of fasting.

It is truly right and just, our duty and our salvation,

always and everywhere to give you thanks,

Lord, holy Father, almighty and eternal God.

For through bodily fasting you restrain our faults,

raise up our minds,

and bestow both virtue and its rewards,

through Christ our Lord.

Through him the Angels praise your majesty,

Dominions adore and Powers tremble before you.

Heaven and the Virtues of heaven and the blessed Seraphim

worship together with exultation.

May our voices, we pray, join with theirs

in humble praise, as we acclaim:

The Priest concludes the Preface with the people singing or saying aloud:

Holy, Holy, Holy Lord God of hosts.

Heaven and earth are full of your glory.

Hosanna in the highest.

Blessed is he who comes in the name of the Lord.

Hosanna in the highest.

After the singing of the Sanctus the congregation kneels for the remainder of the Eucharistic Prayer.

Preface of the Epiphany of the Lord

Christ the light of the nations

The following Preface is said in Masses of the Solemnity of the Epiphany. This Preface, or one of the Prefaces of the Nativity, may be said even on days after the Epiphany up to the Saturday that precedes the Feast of the Baptism of the Lord.

It is truly right and just, our duty and our salvation,

always and everywhere to give you thanks,

Lord, holy Father, almighty and eternal God.

For today you have revealed the mystery

of our salvation in Christ

as a light for the nations,

and, when he appeared in our mortal nature,

you made us new by the glory of his immortal nature.

92

And so, with Angels and Archangels,

with Thrones and Dominions,

and with all the hosts and Powers of heaven,

we sing the hymn of your glory,

as without end we acclaim:

The Priest concludes the Preface with the people singing or saying aloud:

Holy, Holy, Holy Lord God of hosts.

Heaven and earth are full of your glory.

Hosanna in the highest.

Blessed is he who comes in the name of the Lord.

Hosanna in the highest.

After the singing of the Sanctus the congregation kneels for the remainder of the Eucharistic Prayer.

Preface I of the Nativity of the Lord
Christ the Light

The following Preface is said in Masses of the Nativity of the Lord and of its Octave Day, and within the Octave, even in Masses that otherwise might have a proper Preface, with the exception of Masses that have a proper Preface concerning the divine mysteries or divine Persons. It is also used on weekdays of Christmas Time.

It is truly right and just, our duty and our salvation,

always and everywhere to give you thanks,

Lord, holy Father, almighty and eternal God.

For in the mystery of the Word made flesh

a new light of your glory has shone upon the eyes of our mind,

so that, as we recognize in him God made visible,

we may be caught up through him in love of things invisible.

And so, with Angels and Archangels,

with Thrones and Dominions,

and with all the hosts and Powers of heaven,

we sing the hymn of your glory,

as without end we acclaim:

The Priest concludes the Preface with the people singing or saying aloud:

Holy, Holy, Holy Lord God of hosts.

Heaven and earth are full of your glory.

Hosanna in the highest.

Blessed is he who comes in the name of the Lord.

Hosanna in the highest.

After the singing of the Sanctus the congregation kneels for the remainder of the Eucharistic Prayer.

Preface II of the Nativity of the Lord

The restoration of all things in the Incarnation

The following Preface is said in Masses of the Nativity of the Lord and of its Octave Day, and within the Octave, even in Masses that otherwise might have a proper Preface, with the exception of Masses that have a proper Preface concerning the divine mysteries or divine Persons. It is also used on weekdays of Christmas Time.

It is truly right and just, our duty and our salvation,

always and everywhere to give you thanks,

Lord, holy Father, almighty and eternal God,

through Christ our Lord.

For on the feast of this awe-filled mystery,

though invisible in his own divine nature,

he has appeared visibly in ours;

and begotten before all ages,

he has begun to exist in time;

so that, raising up in himself all that was cast down,

he might restore unity to all creation

and call straying humanity back to the heavenly Kingdom.

And so, with all the Angels, we praise you,

as in joyful celebration we acclaim:

The Priest concludes the Preface with the people singing or saying aloud:

Holy, Holy, Holy Lord God of hosts.

Heaven and earth are full of your glory.

Hosanna in the highest.

Blessed is he who comes in the name of the Lord.

Hosanna in the highest.

After the singing of the Sanctus the congregation kneels for the remainder of the Eucharistic Prayer.

Preface III of the Nativity of the Lord

The exchange in the Incarnation of the Word

The following Preface is said in Masses of the Nativity of the Lord and of its Octave Day, and within the Octave, even in Masses that otherwise might have a proper Preface, with the exception of Masses that have a proper Preface concerning the divine mysteries or divine Persons. It is also used on weekdays of Christmas Time.

It is truly right and just, our duty and our salvation,

always and everywhere to give you thanks,

Lord, holy Father, almighty and eternal God,

through Christ our Lord.

For through him the holy exchange that restores our life

has shone forth today in splendour:

when our frailty is assumed by your Word

not only does human mortality receive unending honour

but by this wondrous union we, too, are made eternal.

And so, in company with the choirs of Angels,

we praise you, and with joy we proclaim:

The Priest concludes the Preface with the people singing or saying aloud:

Holy, Holy, Holy Lord God of hosts.

Heaven and earth are full of your glory.

Hosanna in the highest.

Blessed is he who comes in the name of the Lord.

Hosanna in the highest.

After the singing of the Sanctus the congregation kneels for the remainder of the Eucharistic Prayer.

Preface I of Advent

The two comings of Christ

The following Preface is said in Masses of Advent from the First Sunday of Advent to 16 December and in other Masses that are celebrated in Advent and have no proper Preface.

It is truly right and just, our duty and our salvation,

always and everywhere to give you thanks,

Lord, holy Father, almighty and eternal God,

through Christ our Lord.

For he assumed at his first coming

the lowliness of human flesh,

and so fulfilled the design you formed long ago,

and opened for us the way to eternal salvation,

that, when he comes again in glory and majesty

and all is at last made manifest,

we who watch for that day

may inherit the great promise

in which now we dare to hope.

And so, with Angels and Archangels,

with Thrones and Dominions,

and with all the hosts and Powers of heaven,

we sing the hymn of your glory,

as without end we acclaim:

The Priest concludes the Preface with the people singing or saying aloud:

Holy, Holy, Holy Lord God of hosts.

Heaven and earth are full of your glory.

Hosanna in the highest.

Blessed is he who comes in the name of the Lord.

Hosanna in the highest.

After the singing of the Sanctus the congregation kneels for the remainder of the Eucharistic Prayer.

Preface II of Advent

The twofold expectation of Christ

The following Preface is said in Masses of Advent from 17 December to 24 December and in other Masses that are celebrated in Advent and have no proper Preface.

It is truly right and just, our duty and our salvation,

always and everywhere to give you thanks,

Lord, holy Father, almighty and eternal God,

through Christ our Lord.

For all the oracles of the prophets foretold him,

the Virgin Mother longed for him

with love beyond all telling,

John the Baptist sang of his coming

and proclaimed his presence when he came.

It is by his gift that already we rejoice

at the mystery of his Nativity,

so that he may find us watchful in prayer

and exultant in his praise.

And so, with Angels and Archangels,

with Thrones and Dominions,

and with all the hosts and Powers of heaven,

we sing the hymn of your glory,

as without end we acclaim:

The Priest concludes the Preface with the people singing or saying aloud:

Holy, Holy, Holy Lord God of hosts.

Heaven and earth are full of your glory.

Hosanna in the highest.

Blessed is he who comes in the name of the Lord.

Hosanna in the highest.

After the singing of the Sanctus the congregation kneels for the remainder of the Eucharistic Prayer.

Preface I of Saints

The glory of the Saints

The following Preface is said in Masses of All Saints, of Patron Saints and of Saints who are Titulars of a church, and on Solemnities and Feasts of Saints, unless a proper Preface is to be said. This Preface may be said also on Memorials of Saints.

It is truly right and just, our duty and our salvation,

always and everywhere to give you thanks,

Lord, holy Father, almighty and eternal God.

For you are praised in the company of your Saints

and, in crowning their merits, you crown your own gifts.

By their way of life you offer us an example,

by communion with them you give us companionship,

by their intercession, sure support,

so that, encouraged by so great a cloud of witnesses,

we may run as victors in the race before us

and win with them the imperishable crown of glory,

through Christ our Lord.

And so, with the Angels and Archangels,

and with the great multitude of the Saints,

we sing the hymn of your praise,

as without end we acclaim:

The Priest concludes the Preface with the people singing or saying aloud:

Holy, Holy, Holy Lord God of hosts.

Heaven and earth are full of your glory.

Hosanna in the highest.

Blessed is he who comes in the name of the Lord.

Hosanna in the highest.

After the singing of the Sanctus the congregation kneels for the remainder of the Eucharistic Prayer.

Preface II of Saints

The glory of the Saints

The following Preface is said in Masses of All Saints, of Patron Saints and of Saints who are Titulars of a church, and on Solemnities and Feasts of Saints, unless a proper Preface is to be said. This Preface may be said also on Memorials of Saints.

It is truly right and just, our duty and our salvation,

always and everywhere to give you thanks,

Lord, holy Father, almighty and eternal God.

For you are praised in the company of your Saints

and, in crowning their merits, you crown your own gifts.

By their way of life you offer us an example,

by communion with them you give us companionship,

by their intercession, sure support,

so that, encouraged by so great a cloud of witnesses,

we may run as victors in the race before us

and win with them the imperishable crown of glory,

through Christ our Lord.

And so, with the Angels and Archangels,

and with the great multitude of the Saints,

we sing the hymn of your praise,

as without end we acclaim:

The Priest concludes the Preface with the people singing or saying aloud:

Holy, Holy, Holy Lord God of hosts.

Heaven and earth are full of your glory.

Hosanna in the highest.

Blessed is he who comes in the name of the Lord.

Hosanna in the highest.

After the singing of the Sanctus the congregation kneels for the remainder of the Eucharistic Prayer.

Preface II of Saints

The action of the Saints

The following Preface is said in Masses of All Saints, of Patron Saints and of Saints who are Titulars of a church, and on Solemnities and Feasts of Saints, unless a proper Preface is to be said. This Preface may be said also on Memorials of Saints.

It is truly right and just, our duty and our salvation,

always and everywhere to give you thanks,

Lord, holy Father, almighty and eternal God,

through Christ our Lord.

For in the marvellous confession of your Saints,

you make your Church fruitful with strength ever new

and offer us sure signs of your love.

And that your saving mysteries may be fulfilled,

their great example lends us courage,

their fervent prayers sustain us in all we do.

And so, Lord, with all the Angels and Saints,

we, too, give you thanks, as in exultation we acclaim:

The Priest concludes the Preface with the people singing or saying aloud:

Holy, Holy, Holy Lord God of hosts.

Heaven and earth are full of your glory.

Hosanna in the highest.

Blessed is he who comes in the name of the Lord.

Hosanna in the highest.

After the singing of the Sanctus the congregation kneels for the remainder of the Eucharistic Prayer.

Preface of II Holy Martyrs
The wonders of God in the victory of the Martyrs

The following Preface is said on the Solemnities and Feasts of Holy Martyrs. It may also be said on their Memorials.

It is truly right and just, our duty and our salvation,

always and everywhere to give you thanks,

Lord, holy Father, almighty and eternal God.

For you are glorified when your Saints are praised;

their very sufferings are but wonders of your might:

in your mercy you give ardour to their faith,

to their endurance you grant firm resolve,

and in their struggle the victory is yours,

through Christ our Lord.

Therefore, all creatures of heaven and earth

sing a new song in adoration,

and we, with all the host of Angels,

cry out, and without end we acclaim:

The Priest concludes the Preface with the people singing or saying aloud:

Holy, Holy, Holy Lord God of hosts.

Heaven and earth are full of your glory.

Hosanna in the highest.

Blessed is he who comes in the name of the Lord.

Hosanna in the highest.

After the singing of the Sanctus the congregation kneels for the remainder of the Eucharistic Prayer.

Preface of Holy Virgins and Religious

The sign of a life consecrated to God

The following Preface is said on the Solemnities and Feasts of Holy Virgins and Religious. It may also be said on their Memorials.

It is truly right and just, our duty and our salvation,

always and everywhere to give you thanks,

Lord, holy Father, almighty and eternal God.

For in the Saints who consecrated themselves to Christ

for the sake of the Kingdom of Heaven,

it is right to celebrate the wonders of your providence,

by which you call human nature back to its original holiness

and bring it to experience on this earth

the gifts you promise in the new world to come.

And so, with all the Angels and Saints,

we praise you, as without end we acclaim:

The Priest concludes the Preface with the people singing or saying aloud:

Holy, Holy, Holy Lord God of hosts.

Heaven and earth are full of your glory.

Hosanna in the highest.

Blessed is he who comes in the name of the Lord.

Hosanna in the highest.

After the singing of the Sanctus the congregation kneels for the remainder of the Eucharistic Prayer.

Eucharistic Prayer III

The Priest alone says:

You are indeed Holy, O Lord,

and all you have created

rightly gives you praise,

for through your Son our Lord Jesus Christ,

by the power and working of the Holy Spirit,

you give life to all things and make them holy,

and you never cease to gather a people to yourself,

so that from the rising of the sun to its setting

a pure sacrifice may be offered to your name.

Therefore, O Lord, we humbly implore you:

by the same Spirit graciously make holy

these gifts we have brought to you for consecration,

that they may become the Body and ✠ *Blood*

of your Son our Lord Jesus Christ,

at whose command we celebrate these mysteries.

For on the night he was betrayed

he himself took bread,

and, giving you thanks, he said the blessing,

broke the bread and gave it to his disciples, saying:

Take this, all of you, and eat of it,

for this is my Body,

which will be given up for you.

In a similar way, when supper was ended,

he took the chalice,

and, giving you thanks, he said the blessing,

and gave the chalice to his disciples, saying:

Take this, all of you, and drink from it,

for this is the chalice of my Blood,

the Blood of the new and eternal covenant,

which will be poured out for you and for many

for the forgiveness of sins.

Do this in memory of me.

After the words of Consecration the priest says:

The mystery of faith.

The people continue, acclaiming:

Either:

We proclaim your Death, O Lord,

and profess your Resurrection

until you come again.

Or:

When we eat this Bread and drink this Cup,

we proclaim your Death, O Lord,

until you come again.

Or:

Save us, Saviour of the world,

for by your Cross and Resurrection

you have set us free.

Then the Priest alone continues:

Therefore, O Lord, as we celebrate the memorial

of the saving Passion of your Son,

his wondrous Resurrection

and Ascension into heaven,

and as we look forward to his second coming,

we offer you in thanksgiving

this holy and living sacrifice.

Look, we pray, upon the oblation of your Church

and, recognizing the sacrificial Victim by whose death

you willed to reconcile us to yourself,

grant that we, who are nourished

by the Body and Blood of your Son

and filled with his Holy Spirit,

may become one body, one spirit in Christ.

May he make of us

an eternal offering to you,

so that we may obtain an inheritance with your elect,

especially with the most Blessed Virgin Mary, Mother of God,

with blessed Joseph, her Spouse,

with your blessed Apostles and glorious Martyrs

(with Saint N.: the Saint of the day or Patron Saint)

and with all the Saints,

on whose constant intercession in your presence

we rely for unfailing help.

May this Sacrifice of our reconciliation,

we pray, O Lord,

advance the peace and salvation of all the world.

Be pleased to confirm in faith and charity

your pilgrim Church on earth,

with your servant N. our Pope and N. our Bishop,

the Order of Bishops, all the clergy,

and the entire people you have gained for your own.

Listen graciously to the prayers of this family,

whom you have summoned before you:

in your compassion, O merciful Father,

gather to yourself all your children

scattered throughout the world.

To our departed brothers and sisters

and to all who were pleasing to you

at their passing from this life,

give kind admittance to your kingdom.

There we hope to enjoy for ever the fullness of your glory

through Christ our Lord,

through whom you bestow on the world all that is good.

When this Eucharistic Prayer is used in Masses for the
Dead, the following may be said instead:
Remember your servant N.
whom you have called (today)
from this world to yourself.
Grant that he (she) who was united with your Son in a
death like his,
may also be one with him in his Resurrection,
when from the earth
he will raise up in the flesh those who have died,
and transform our lowly body
after the pattern of his own glorious body.

To our departed brothers and sisters, too,
and to all who were pleasing to you
at their passing from this life,
give kind admittance to your kingdom.
There we hope to enjoy for ever the fullness of your
glory,
when you will wipe away every tear from our eyes.
For seeing you, our God, as you are,
we shall be like you for all the ages
and praise you without end,
through Christ our Lord,
through whom you bestow on the world all that is good.

At the conclusion of the Eucharistic Prayer the Priest takes the
chalice and the paten with the host and, raising both, he alone
says:

Through him, and with him, and in him,

O God, almighty Father,

in the unity of the Holy Spirit,

all glory and honour is yours,

for ever and ever.

Amen.

Eucharistic Prayer IV

The Priest alone says:

We give you praise, Father most holy,

for you are great

and you have fashioned all your works

in wisdom and in love.

You formed man in your own image

and entrusted the whole world to his care,

so that in serving you alone, the Creator,

he might have dominion over all creatures.

And when through disobedience he had lost your friendship,

you did not abandon him to the domain of death.

For you came in mercy to the aid of all,

so that those who seek might find you.

Time and again you offered them covenants

and through the prophets

taught them to look forward to salvation.

And you so loved the world, Father most holy,

that in the fullness of time

you sent your Only Begotten Son to be our Saviour.

Made incarnate by the Holy Spirit

and born of the Virgin Mary,

he shared our human nature

in all things but sin.

To the poor he proclaimed the good news of salvation,

to prisoners, freedom,

and to the sorrowful of heart, joy.

To accomplish your plan,

he gave himself up to death,

and, rising from the dead,

he destroyed death and restored life.

And that we might live no longer for ourselves

but for him who died and rose again for us,

he sent the Holy Spirit from you, Father,

as the first fruits for those who believe,

so that, bringing to perfection his work in the world,

he might sanctify creation to the full.

Therefore, O Lord, we pray:

may this same Holy Spirit

graciously sanctify these offerings,

that they may become

the Body and ✠ Blood of our Lord Jesus Christ

for the celebration of this great mystery,

which he himself left us

as an eternal covenant.

For when the hour had come

for him to be glorified by you, Father most holy,

having loved his own who were in the world,

he loved them to the end:

and while they were at supper,

he took bread, blessed and broke it,

and gave it to his disciples, saying:

Take this, all of you, and eat of it,

for this is my Body,

which will be given up for you.

In a similar way,

taking the chalice filled with the fruit of the vine,

he gave thanks,

and gave the chalice to his disciples, saying:

Take this, all of you, and drink from it,

for this is the chalice of my Blood,

the Blood of the new and eternal covenant,

which will be poured out for you and for many

for the forgiveness of sins.

Do this in memory of me.

After the words of Consecration the priest says:

The mystery of faith.

The people continue, acclaiming:

Either:

We proclaim your Death, O Lord,

and profess your Resurrection

until you come again.

Or:

When we eat this Bread and drink this Cup,

we proclaim your Death, O Lord,

until you come again.

Or:

Save us, Saviour of the world,

for by your Cross and Resurrection

you have set us free.

Then the Priest alone continues:

Therefore, O Lord,

as we now celebrate the memorial of our redemption,

we remember Christ's Death

and his descent to the realm of the dead,

we proclaim his Resurrection

and his Ascension to your right hand,

and, as we await his coming in glory,

we offer you his Body and Blood,

the sacrifice acceptable to you

which brings salvation to the whole world.

Look, O Lord, upon the Sacrifice

which you yourself have provided for your Church,

and grant in your loving kindness

to all who partake of this one Bread and one Chalice

that, gathered into one body by the Holy Spirit,

they may truly become a living sacrifice in Christ

to the praise of your glory.

Therefore, Lord, remember now

all for whom we offer this sacrifice:

especially your servant N. our Pope,

N. our Bishop, and the whole Order of Bishops,

all the clergy,

those who take part in this offering,

those gathered here before you,

your entire people,

and all who seek you with a sincere heart.

Remember also

those who have died in the peace of your Christ

and all the dead,

whose faith you alone have known.

To all of us, your children,

grant, O merciful Father,

that we may enter into a heavenly inheritance

with the Blessed Virgin Mary, Mother of God,

with blessed Joseph, her Spouse,

and with your Apostles and Saints in your kingdom.

There, with the whole of creation,

freed from the corruption of sin and death,

may we glorify you through Christ our Lord,

through whom you bestow on the world all that is good.

At the conclusion of the Eucharistic Prayer the Priest takes the chalice and the paten with the host and, raising both, he alone says:

Through him, and with him, and in him,

O God, almighty Father,

in the unity of the Holy Spirit,

all glory and honour is yours,

for ever and ever.

Amen.

For Reconciliation I

The Priest alone says:

You are indeed Holy, O Lord,

and from the world's beginning

are ceaselessly at work,

so that the human race may become holy,

just as you yourself are holy.

Look, we pray, upon your people's offerings
and pour out on them the power of your Spirit,
that they may become the Body and ✠ *Blood*
of your beloved Son, Jesus Christ,
in whom we, too, are your sons and daughters.

Indeed, though we once were lost
and could not approach you,
you loved us with the greatest love:
for your Son, who alone is just,
handed himself over to death,
and did not disdain to be nailed for our sake
to the wood of the Cross.

But before his arms were outstretched between heaven and earth,
to become the lasting sign of your covenant,
he desired to celebrate the Passover with his disciples.

As he ate with them,
he took bread

and, giving you thanks, he said the blessing,

broke the bread and gave it to them, saying:

Take this, all of you, and eat of it,

for this is my Body,

which will be given up for you.

In a similar way, when supper was ended,

knowing that he was about to reconcile all things in himself

through his Blood to be shed on the Cross,

he took the chalice, filled with the fruit of the vine,

and once more giving you thanks,

handed the chalice to his disciples, saying:

Take this, all of you, and drink from it,

for this is the chalice of my Blood,

the Blood of the new and eternal covenant,

which will be poured out for you and for many

for the forgiveness of sins.

Do this in memory of me.

After the words of Consecration the priest says:

The mystery of faith.

The people continue, acclaiming:

Either:

We proclaim your Death, O Lord,

and profess your Resurrection

until you come again.

Or:

When we eat this Bread and drink this Cup,

we proclaim your Death, O Lord,

until you come again.

Or:

Save us, Saviour of the world,

for by your Cross and Resurrection

you have set us free.

Then the Priest alone continues:

Therefore, as we celebrate

the memorial of your Son Jesus Christ,

who is our Passover and our surest peace,

we celebrate his Death and Resurrection from the dead,

and looking forward to his blessed Coming,

we offer you, who are our faithful and merciful God,

this sacrificial Victim

who reconciles to you the human race.

Look kindly, most compassionate Father,

on those you unite to yourself

by the Sacrifice of your Son,

and grant that, by the power of the Holy Spirit,

as they partake of this one Bread and one Chalice,

they may be gathered into one Body in Christ,

who heals every division.

Be pleased to keep us always

in communion of mind and heart,

together with N. our Pope and N. our Bishop.

Help us to work together

for the coming of your Kingdom,

until the hour when we stand before you,

Saints among the Saints in the halls of heaven,

with the Blessed Virgin Mary, Mother of God,

with blessed Joseph, her Spouse,

the blessed Apostles and all the Saints,

and with our deceased brothers and sisters,

whom we humbly commend to your mercy.

Then, freed at last from the wound of corruption

and made fully into a new creation,

we shall sing to you with gladness

the thanksgiving of Christ,

who lives for all eternity.

At the conclusion of the Eucharistic Prayer the Priest takes the
chalice and the paten with the host and, raising both, he alone
says:

Through him, and with him, and in him,

O God, almighty Father,

in the unity of the Holy Spirit,

all glory and honour is yours,

for ever and ever.

Amen.

For Reconciliation II

The Priest alone says:

You, therefore, almighty Father,

we bless through Jesus Christ your Son,

who comes in your name.

He himself is the Word that brings salvation,

the hand you extend to sinners,

the way by which your peace is offered to us.

When we ourselves had turned away from you

on account of our sins,

you brought us back to be reconciled, O Lord,

so that, converted at last to you,

we might love one another

through your Son,

whom for our sake you handed over to death.

And now, celebrating the reconciliation

Christ has brought us,

we entreat you:

sanctify these gifts by the outpouring of your Spirit,

that they may become the Body and ✠ *Blood of your Son,*

whose command we fulfil

when we celebrate these mysteries.

For when about to give his life to set us free,

as he reclined at supper,

he himself took bread into his hands,

and, giving you thanks, he said the blessing,

broke the bread and gave it to his disciples, saying:

Take this, all of you, and eat of it,

for this is my Body,

which will be given up for you.

In a similar way, on that same evening,

he took the chalice of blessing in his hands,

confessing your mercy,

and gave the chalice to his disciples, saying:

Take this, all of you, and drink from it,

for this is the chalice of my Blood,

the Blood of the new and eternal covenant,

which will be poured out for you and for many

for the forgiveness of sins.

Do this in memory of me.

After the words of Consecration the priest says:

The mystery of faith.

The people continue, acclaiming:

Either:

We proclaim your Death, O Lord,

and profess your Resurrection

until you come again.

Or:

When we eat this Bread and drink this Cup,

we proclaim your Death, O Lord,

until you come again.

Or:

Save us, Saviour of the world,

for by your Cross and Resurrection

you have set us free.

Then the Priest alone continues:

Celebrating, therefore, the memorial

of the Death and Resurrection of your Son,

who left us this pledge of his love,

we offer you what you have bestowed on us,

the Sacrifice of perfect reconciliation.

Holy Father, we humbly beseech you

to accept us also, together with your Son,

and in this saving banquet

graciously to endow us with his very Spirit,

who takes away everything

that estranges us from one another.

May he make your Church a sign of unity

and an instrument of your peace among all people

and may he keep us in communion

with N. our Pope and N. our Bishop

and all the Bishops

and your entire people.

Just as you have gathered us now at the table of your Son,

so also bring us together,

with the glorious Virgin Mary, Mother of God,

with blessed Joseph, her Spouse,

with your blessed Apostles and all the Saints,

with our brothers and sisters

and those of every race and tongue

who have died in your friendship.

Bring us to share with them the unending banquet of unity

in a new heaven and a new earth,

where the fullness of your peace will shine forth

in Christ Jesus our Lord.

At the conclusion of the Eucharistic Prayer the Priest takes the chalice and the paten with the host and, raising both, he alone says:

Through him, and with him, and in him,

O God, almighty Father,

in the unity of the Holy Spirit,

all glory and honour is yours,

for ever and ever.

Amen.

For Various Needs I

The Priest alone says:

You are indeed Holy and to be glorified, O God,

who love the human race

and who always walk with us on the journey of life.

Blessed indeed is your Son,

present in our midst

when we are gathered by his love,

and when, as once for the disciples, so now for us,

he opens the Scriptures and breaks the bread.

Therefore, Father most merciful,

we ask that you send forth your Holy Spirit

to sanctify these gifts of bread and wine,

that they may become for us

the Body and ✠ *Blood*

of our Lord Jesus Christ.

On the day before he was to suffer,

on the night of the Last Supper,

he took bread and said the blessing,

broke the bread and gave it to his disciples, saying:

Take this, all of you, and eat of it,

for this is my Body,

which will be given up for you.

In a similar way, when supper was ended,

he took the chalice, gave you thanks

and gave the chalice to his disciples, saying:

Take this, all of you, and drink from it,

for this is the chalice of my Blood,

the Blood of the new and eternal covenant,

which will be poured out for you and for many

for the forgiveness of sins.

Do this in memory of me.

After the words of Consecration the priest says:

The mystery of faith.

The people continue, acclaiming:

Either:

We proclaim your Death, O Lord,

and profess your Resurrection

until you come again.

Or:

When we eat this Bread and drink this Cup,

we proclaim your Death, O Lord,

until you come again.

Or:

Save us, Saviour of the world,

for by your Cross and Resurrection

you have set us free.

Then the Priest alone continues:

Therefore, holy Father,

as we celebrate the memorial of Christ your Son, our Saviour,

whom you led through his Passion and Death on the Cross

to the glory of the Resurrection,

and whom you have seated at your right hand,

we proclaim the work of your love until he comes again

and we offer you the Bread of life

and the Chalice of blessing.

Look with favour on the oblation of your Church,

in which we show forth

the paschal Sacrifice of Christ that has been handed on to us,

and grant that, by the power of the Spirit of your love,

we may be counted now and until the day of eternity

among the members of your Son,

in whose Body and Blood we have communion.

Lord, renew your Church (which is in N.)

by the light of the Gospel.

Strengthen the bond of unity

between the faithful and the pastors of your people,

together with N. our Pope, N. our Bishop,

and the whole Order of Bishops,

that in a world torn by strife

your people may shine forth

as a prophetic sign of unity and concord.

Remember our brothers and sisters (N. and N.),

who have fallen asleep in the peace of your Christ,

and all the dead, whose faith you alone have known.

Admit them to rejoice in the light of your face,

and in the resurrection give them the fullness of life.

Grant also to us,

when our earthly pilgrimage is done,

that we may come to an eternal dwelling place

and live with you for ever;

there, in communion with the Blessed Virgin Mary, Mother of God,

with blessed Joseph, her Spouse,

with the Apostles and Martyrs,

(with Saint N.: the Saint of the day or Patron)

and with all the Saints,

we shall praise and exalt you

through Jesus Christ, your Son.

At the conclusion of the Eucharistic Prayer the Priest takes the chalice and the paten with the host and, raising both, he alone says:

Through him, and with him, and in him,

O God, almighty Father,

in the unity of the Holy Spirit,

all glory and honour is yours,

for ever and ever.

Amen.

The Priest alone says:

You are indeed Holy and to be glorified, O God,

who love the human race

and who always walk with us on the journey of life.

Blessed indeed is your Son,

present in our midst

when we are gathered by his love,

and when, as once for the disciples, so now for us,

he opens the Scriptures and breaks the bread.

Therefore, Father most merciful,

we ask that you send forth your Holy Spirit

to sanctify these gifts of bread and wine,

that they may become for us

the Body and ✠ Blood

of our Lord Jesus Christ.

On the day before he was to suffer,

on the night of the Last Supper,

he took bread and said the blessing,

broke the bread and gave it to his disciples, saying:

Take this, all of you, and eat of it,

for this is my Body,

which will be given up for you.

In a similar way, when supper was ended,

he took the chalice, gave you thanks

and gave the chalice to his disciples, saying:

Take this, all of you, and drink from it,

for this is the chalice of my Blood,

the Blood of the new and eternal covenant,

which will be poured out for you and for many

for the forgiveness of sins.

Do this in memory of me.

After the words of Consecration the priest says:

The mystery of faith.

The people continue, acclaiming:

Either:

We proclaim your Death, O Lord,

and profess your Resurrection

until you come again.

Or:

When we eat this Bread and drink this Cup,

we proclaim your Death, O Lord,

until you come again.

Or:

Save us, Saviour of the world,

for by your Cross and Resurrection

you have set us free.

Then the Priest alone continues:

Therefore, holy Father,

as we celebrate the memorial of Christ your Son, our Saviour,

whom you led through his Passion and Death on the Cross

to the glory of the Resurrection,

and whom you have seated at your right hand,

we proclaim the work of your love until he comes again

and we offer you the Bread of life

and the Chalice of blessing.

Look with favour on the oblation of your Church,

in which we show forth

the paschal Sacrifice of Christ that has been handed on to us,

and grant that, by the power of the Spirit of your love,

we may be counted now and until the day of eternity

among the members of your Son,

in whose Body and Blood we have communion.

Lord, renew your Church (which is in N.)

by the light of the Gospel.

Strengthen the bond of unity

between the faithful and the pastors of your people,

together with N. our Pope, N. our Bishop,

and the whole Order of Bishops,

that in a world torn by strife

your people may shine forth

as a prophetic sign of unity and concord.

Remember our brothers and sisters (N. and N.),

who have fallen asleep in the peace of your Christ,

and all the dead, whose faith you alone have known.

Admit them to rejoice in the light of your face,

and in the resurrection give them the fullness of life.

Grant also to us,

when our earthly pilgrimage is done,

that we may come to an eternal dwelling place

and live with you for ever;

there, in communion with the Blessed Virgin Mary, Mother of God,

with blessed Joseph, her Spouse,

with the Apostles and Martyrs,

(with Saint N.: the Saint of the day or Patron)

and with all the Saints,

we shall praise and exalt you

through Jesus Christ, your Son.

At the conclusion of the Eucharistic Prayer the Priest takes the chalice and the paten with the host and, raising both, he alone says:

Through him, and with him, and in him,

O God, almighty Father,

in the unity of the Holy Spirit,

all glory and honour is yours,

for ever and ever.

Amen.

For Various Needs III

The Priest alone says:

You are indeed Holy and to be glorified, O God,

who love the human race

and who always walk with us on the journey of life.

Blessed indeed is your Son,

present in our midst

when we are gathered by his love,

and when, as once for the disciples, so now for us,

he opens the Scriptures and breaks the bread.

Therefore, Father most merciful,

we ask that you send forth your Holy Spirit

to sanctify these gifts of bread and wine,

that they may become for us

the Body and ✠ Blood

of our Lord Jesus Christ.

On the day before he was to suffer,

on the night of the Last Supper,

he took bread and said the blessing,

broke the bread and gave it to his disciples, saying:

Take this, all of you, and eat of it,

for this is my Body,

which will be given up for you.

In a similar way, when supper was ended,

he took the chalice, gave you thanks

and gave the chalice to his disciples, saying:

Take this, all of you, and drink from it,

for this is the chalice of my Blood,

the Blood of the new and eternal covenant,

which will be poured out for you and for many

for the forgiveness of sins.

Do this in memory of me.

After the words of Consecration the priest says:

The mystery of faith.

The people continue, acclaiming:

Either:

We proclaim your Death, O Lord,

and profess your Resurrection

until you come again.

Or:

When we eat this Bread and drink this Cup,

we proclaim your Death, O Lord,

until you come again.

Or:

Save us, Saviour of the world,

for by your Cross and Resurrection

you have set us free.

Then the Priest alone continues:

Therefore, holy Father,

as we celebrate the memorial of Christ your Son, our Saviour, whom you led through his Passion and Death on the Cross

to the glory of the Resurrection,

and whom you have seated at your right hand,

we proclaim the work of your love until he comes again

and we offer you the Bread of life

and the Chalice of blessing.

Look with favour on the oblation of your Church,

in which we show forth

the paschal Sacrifice of Christ that has been handed on to us,

and grant that, by the power of the Spirit of your love,

we may be counted now and until the day of eternity

among the members of your Son,

in whose Body and Blood we have communion.

By our partaking of this mystery, almighty Father,

give us life through your Spirit,

grant that we may be conformed to the image of your Son,

and confirm us in the bond of communion,

together with N. our Pope and N. our Bishop,

with all other Bishops,

with Priests and Deacons,

and with your entire people.

Grant that all the faithful of the Church,

looking into the signs of the times by the light of faith,

may constantly devote themselves

to the service of the Gospel.

Keep us attentive to the needs of all

that, sharing their grief and pain,

their joy and hope,

we may faithfully bring them the good news of salvation

and go forward with them

along the way of your Kingdom.

Remember our brothers and sisters (N. and N.),

who have fallen asleep in the peace of your Christ,

and all the dead, whose faith you alone have known.

Admit them to rejoice in the light of your face,

and in the resurrection give them the fullness of life.

Grant also to us,

when our earthly pilgrimage is done,

that we may come to an eternal dwelling place

and live with you for ever;

there, in communion with the Blessed Virgin Mary, Mother of God,

with blessed Joseph, her Spouse,

with the Apostles and Martyrs,

(with Saint N.: the Saint of the day or Patron)

and with all the Saints,

we shall praise and exalt you

through Jesus Christ, your Son.

At the conclusion of the Eucharistic Prayer the Priest takes the chalice and the paten with the host and, raising both, he alone says:

Through him, and with him, and in him,

O God, almighty Father,

in the unity of the Holy Spirit,

all glory and honour is yours,

for ever and ever.

Amen.

For Various Needs IV

The Priest alone says:

You are indeed Holy and to be glorified, O God,

who love the human race

and who always walk with us on the journey of life.

Blessed indeed is your Son,

present in our midst

when we are gathered by his love,

and when, as once for the disciples, so now for us,

he opens the Scriptures and breaks the bread.

Therefore, Father most merciful,

we ask that you send forth your Holy Spirit

to sanctify these gifts of bread and wine,

that they may become for us

the Body and ✠ Blood

of our Lord Jesus Christ.

On the day before he was to suffer,

on the night of the Last Supper,

he took bread and said the blessing,

broke the bread and gave it to his disciples, saying:

Take this, all of you, and eat of it,

for this is my Body,

which will be given up for you.

In a similar way, when supper was ended,

he took the chalice, gave you thanks

and gave the chalice to his disciples, saying:

Take this, all of you, and drink from it,

for this is the chalice of my Blood,

the Blood of the new and eternal covenant,

which will be poured out for you and for many

for the forgiveness of sins.

Do this in memory of me.

After the words of Consecration the priest says:

The mystery of faith.

The people continue, acclaiming:

Either:

We proclaim your Death, O Lord,

and profess your Resurrection

until you come again.

Or:

When we eat this Bread and drink this Cup,

we proclaim your Death, O Lord,

until you come again.

Or:

Save us, Saviour of the world,

for by your Cross and Resurrection

you have set us free.

Then the Priest alone continues:

Therefore, holy Father,

as we celebrate the memorial of Christ your Son, our Saviour,

whom you led through his Passion and Death on the Cross

to the glory of the Resurrection,

and whom you have seated at your right hand,

we proclaim the work of your love until he comes again

and we offer you the Bread of life

and the Chalice of blessing.

Look with favour on the oblation of your Church,

in which we show forth

the paschal Sacrifice of Christ that has been handed on to us,

and grant that, by the power of the Spirit of your love,

we may be counted now and until the day of eternity

among the members of your Son,

in whose Body and Blood we have communion.

Bring your Church, O Lord,

to perfect faith and charity,

together with N. our Pope and N. our Bishop,

with all Bishops, Priests and Deacons,

and the entire people you have made your own.

Open our eyes

to the needs of our brothers and sisters;

inspire in us words and actions

to comfort those who labour and are burdened.

Make us serve them truly,

after the example of Christ and at his command.

And may your Church stand as a living witness

to truth and freedom,

to peace and justice,

that all people may be raised up to a new hope.

151

*Remember our brothers and sisters (*N. *and* N.*),*

who have fallen asleep in the peace of your Christ,

and all the dead, whose faith you alone have known.

Admit them to rejoice in the light of your face,

and in the resurrection give them the fullness of life.

Grant also to us,

when our earthly pilgrimage is done,

that we may come to an eternal dwelling place

and live with you for ever;

there, in communion with the Blessed Virgin Mary, Mother of God,

with blessed Joseph, her Spouse,

with the Apostles and Martyrs,

(with Saint N.: the Saint of the day or Patron)

and with all the Saints,

we shall praise and exalt you

through Jesus Christ, your Son.

At the conclusion of the Eucharistic Prayer the Priest takes the chalice and the paten with the host and, raising both, he alone says:

Through him, and with him, and in him,

O God, almighty Father,

in the unity of the Holy Spirit,

all glory and honour is yours,

for ever and ever.

Amen.

Show only the people's part

After the words of Consecration the priest says:

The mystery of faith.

The people continue, acclaiming:

Either:

We proclaim your Death, O Lord,

and profess your Resurrection

until you come again.

Or:

When we eat this Bread and drink this Cup,

we proclaim your Death, O Lord,

until you come again.

Or:

Save us, Saviour of the world,

153

for by your Cross and Resurrection

you have set us free.

At the conclusion of the Eucharistic Prayer the Priest takes the chalice and the paten with the host and, raising both, he alone says:

Through him, and with him, and in him,

O God, almighty Father,

in the unity of the Holy Spirit,

all glory and honour is yours,

for ever and ever.

Amen.

The Communion Rite

The eating and drinking together of the Lord's Body and Blood in a Paschal meal is the culmination of the Eucharist. The themes underlying these rites are the mutual love and reconciliation that are both the condition and the fruit of worthy communion and the unity of the many in the One.

The Lord's Prayer

The congregation stands and the Priest says:

At the Saviour's command

and formed by divine teaching, we dare to say:

Together with the people, he continues:

Our Father, who art in heaven,

hallowed be thy name;

thy kingdom come,

thy will be done

on earth as it is in heaven.

Give us this day our daily bread,

and forgive us our trespasses,

as we forgive those who trespass against us;

and lead us not into temptation,

but deliver us from evil.

The Priest alone continues, saying:

Deliver us, Lord, we pray, from every evil,

graciously grant peace in our days,

that, by the help of your mercy,

we may be always free from sin

and safe from all distress,

as we await the blessed hope

and the coming of our Saviour, Jesus Christ.

The people conclude the prayer, acclaiming:

For the kingdom,

the power and the glory are yours

now and for ever.

Then the Priest alone says aloud:

Lord Jesus Christ,

who said to your Apostles:

Peace I leave you, my peace I give you,

look not on our sins,

but on the faith of your Church,

and graciously grant her peace and unity

in accordance with your will.

Who live and reign for ever and ever.

The people reply:

Amen.

The Priest adds:

The peace of the Lord be with you always.

The people reply:

And with your spirit.

The Deacon, or the Priest, adds:

Let us offer each other the sign of peace.

And all offer one another the customary sign of peace: a handclasp or handshake, which is an expression of peace, communion, and charity.

Breaking of the Bread

During the breaking of the host the following is sung or said:

Lamb of God, you take away the sins of the world,

have mercy on us.

Lamb of God, you take away the sins of the world,

have mercy on us.

Lamb of God, you take away the sins of the world,

grant us peace.

After the Lamb of God, the people kneel.

Invitation to Communion

After his private prayers of preparation the Priest genuflects, takes the host and, holding it slightly raised above the paten or above the chalice says aloud:

Behold the Lamb of God,

behold him who takes away the sins of the world.

Blessed are those called to the supper of the Lamb.

And together with the people he adds once:

Lord, I am not worthy

that you should enter under my roof,

but only say the word and my soul shall be healed.

Communion

After the priest has reverently consumed the Body and Blood of Christ the communicants come forward in reverent procession, and make a preparatory act of reverence by bowing their head in honour of Christ's presence in the Sacrament. They receive Holy Communion standing. The Priest says:

The Body (Blood) of Christ.

The communicant replies:

Amen.

When Communion is ministered under both kinds the minister of the Chalice raises it slightly and shows it to each of the communicants, saying:

The Blood of Christ.

The communicant replies:

Amen.

After the distribution of Communion, if appropriate, a sacred silence may be observed for a while, or a psalm or other canticle of praise or a hymn may be sung.

Prayer after Communion

Then, the Priest says:

Let us pray.

All stand and pray in silence. Then the Priest says the Prayer after Communion, at the end of which the people acclaim:

Amen.

The Concluding Rites

The brief Concluding Rite sends the people forth to put into effect in their daily lives the Mystery of Christ's Death and Resurrection and the unity in Christ which they have celebrated. Their mission is to witness to Christ in the world and to bring the Gospel to the poor.

Any brief announcements to the people follow here. Then the dismissal takes place. Sometimes this takes a more elaborate form than that given below.

Blessing

The Priest says:

The Lord be with you.

The people reply:

And with your spirit.

The Priest blesses the people, saying:

May almighty God bless you,

the Father, and the Son, ✠ *and the Holy Spirit.*

The people reply:

Amen.

Dismissal

Then the Deacon, or the Priest himself, says:

Either: *Go forth, the Mass is ended.*

160

Or: *Go and announce the Gospel of the Lord.*

Or: *Go in peace, glorifying the Lord by your life.*

Or: *Go in peace.*

The people reply:

Thanks be to God.

Manufactured by Amazon.ca
Bolton, ON